THE STEP BY STEP ART OF
Table Decorating

CLB 3127
© 1993 Colour Library Books Ltd., Godalming, Surrey, England
All rights reserved
This 1994 edition published by Crescent Books, distributed by
Outlet Book Company, Inc., a Random House Company,
40 Engelhard Avenue, Avenel, New Jersey 07001

Random House
New York • Toronto • London • Sydney • Auckland

Printed and bound in Singapore
ISBN 0 517 08662 X

THE STEP BY STEP ART OF

Table Decorating

Design ideas by
JANE MCDONNELL

Photography by
STEVE TANNER
& NEIL SUTHERLAND

CRESCENT BOOKS
NEW YORK • AVENEL, NEW JERSEY

Contents

Materials and Techniques

The decorations in this book are surprisingly easy to achieve and the techniques have been simplified to enable you to produce stunning table effects with little effort.

BASIC EQUIPMENT

Most of the tools and materials you need can be found around the house or purchased easily from art shops, supermarkets or department stores. Haberdashery departments are a particularly useful source for odd pieces and trimmings that may be difficult to obtain anywhere else, as well as for fabrics and wadding. Choose good quality equipment if possible. This is especially important when buying paintbrushes – if you are not used to painting you need all the help that a small springy brush will give you. Soft squirrel hair brushes are not suitable for the fine control that you will need but there are plenty of artificial hair brushes available in the middle price range.

The same advice applies when choosing a knife. It is far easier to cut out a stencil with a sharp knife than to hack away with a blunt one. The scalpel type used by professional designers can be purchased fairly easily, but a craft knife is excellent for the job and probably safer. However, as soon as you find difficulty in cutting and have to exert extra pressure on the blade, change the blunt blade for a new one. When using a knife always keep your fingers behind the cutting edge.

Select the right type of paint for the job. Art shops sell a wide range of specialist paints that will help you achieve the finished effect you require. Read the instructions on paint jars and tubes carefully before using them – paints and dyes vary in their methods of application.

GETTING STARTED

Do not be put off making something because you have never used that method before. A variety of techniques are presented here, most of which are easily mastered and once learnt can be applied to many projects. For example, stencils are used for decorating a variety of items. Never be worried about trying something out on a piece of rough paper before the final item. You can gain confidence very quickly if you try it first.

Most of the painted designs are available as templates on pages 106-123, but it is easy to trace out your own design from a magazine. The trick is to simplify the shapes by tracing the outlines. You may find it helpful to trace a picture, then trace the tracing, to produce a rougher and simpler shape. Finally, make sure you allow yourself the luxury of enjoying the making of your decorations as much as the finished result. Do not rush or set yourself impossible targets. Be kind to yourself and have fun.

SALT DOUGH

Salt dough is an ideal material with which to model a variety of hanging and table decorations. It can be made in advance and stored in an airtight bag in the fridge or freezer. 75 g (1 lb) flour makes enough dough for a large wreath and several small ones.

Materials
Plain flour
Salt
Water
Airtight plastic bags
Watercolour paints
Varnish

1 *Mix 3 parts plain flour to 3 parts salt with about $1^{1}/_{2}$ parts water, adding the water gradually as necessary. Knead into a flexible dough on a floured board if too sticky. Add a little cooking oil to aid plasticity if necessary.*

2 *To make hanging decorations use the dough like pastry. Roll it out to a thickness of about 1 cm ($^{3}/_{8}$ in). Using a pastry cutter, cut out a circle. Then, using a smaller cutter, cut out the centre piece to make a ring.*

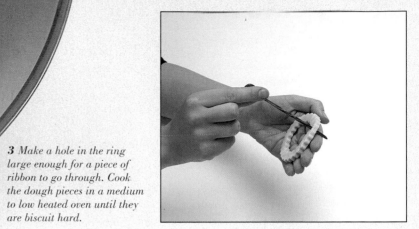

3 *Make a hole in the ring large enough for a piece of ribbon to go through. Cook the dough pieces in a medium to low heated oven until they are biscuit hard.*

4 *Paint the cooked dough pieces with water-based colours. Leave to dry thoroughly before applying a second colour.*

5 *Varnish the pieces for a good gloss. They will be quite hardwearing and will last a long time, if kept away from excessive damp.*

PAINTING ON CHINA AND GLASS

Glass painting colours are available in most art shops. They come in the form of transparent varnishes and dry to an extremely hard finish. You can blend colours together, add white to them to make them opaque or add thinners to produce a delicate washed effect.

China painting colours are similar to those used on glass. In fact, you can use glass paints if china paints are unavailable. True china painting enamels are fired on to china in a kiln and require expert knowledge. With the hardening varnish colours available from art shops, however, you can achieve a surprisingly professional finish, especially on white china.

Materials
Glass paints
China paints (optional)
Spirit marker
Brush
White spirit

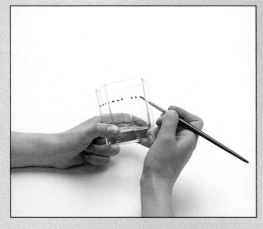

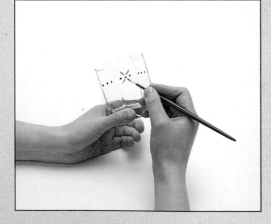

GLASS PAINTING

1 *With all painting techniques plan your pattern first, working out the size and scale of your design to suit the item you want to decorate. Keep the decoration away from the rims of glasses. It is best to use small patterns. You will find that the easiest are based on dots and dashes placed randomly or in an ordered design. Paint dots using the point of the brush.*

2 *Clean the brush well in white spirit. Apply dashes to the glass using long sweeps of the brush.*

CHINA PAINTING

1 *Use a spirit marker to sketch the design on to the china. Do not paint inside eating bowls and keep the decoration away from the rims of cups. If you intend to paint several pieces for a table setting keep the design as simple as possible, perhaps just a border, so that the job does not become too arduous.*

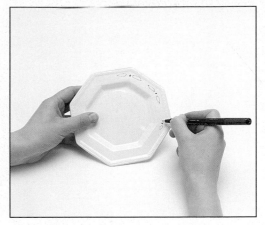

2 *Use the paints sparingly, using simple brush strokes. If they are applied too heavily or in large areas the final effect can look clumsy and overworked.*

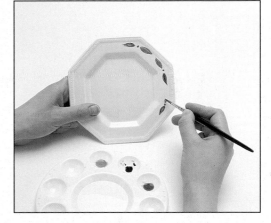

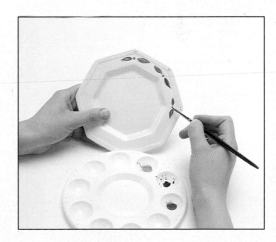

3 *Remember to wash your brush out well in white spirit between colours and when you have finished. The decoration will chip off eventually with use, but can be reapplied.*

STENCILLING

Stencilling gives you the freedom to apply any pattern you like to table items so that you can co-ordinate designs and colours. The technique of applying the inks or paints is simple. Use a small natural sponge for a soft look or a bristle stencil brush for bolder outlines.

Materials
Tracing paper
Pencil
Stencil card
Sharp craft knife
Masking tape
Sponge
Stencil brush

DRAWING AND CUTTING

1 *Trace out the pattern that you require from the template section (on pages 106-123) or design your own.*

2 *If you want to change the scale of the design trace it onto graph paper. Then copy the pattern square by square onto another piece of graph paper. Count the larger squares to enlarge the design and the smaller ones to reduce it in size. Alternatively, you can have your design photocopied and enlarged or reduced mechanically.*

3 *Once your pattern is the size you want, trace the outline on the back with a heavy pencil. Lay it down on the stencil card and retrace it. Following the new outline on the card, cut out the stencil with a craft knife.*

PAINTING A STENCIL
1 *Place the stencil over the item you wish to decorate and secure it lightly with masking tape. Put all your colours out on to saucers. If you are mixing colours make sure that you have enough to complete the whole pattern. Use a stencil brush for a crisp outline.*

2 *Create shading by sponging in another colour or darker tone after the first has dried. Be careful not to overload the brush or sponge so that the paint does not bleed under the edge of the stencil. Aim for a dry look and you will find that the paint is easier to apply and less likely to run. Do not remove the stencil until you have applied all the colours.*

APPLYING PATTERN
TO FABRIC AND PAPER

When stencilling onto fabric use specialist fabric inks and choose them according to the type of fabric you are using. Fabric inks are also available in fibre tip form and are useful for drawing in details. Spirit-based markers dye permanently and can be used for putting in fine lines.

Potato prints are a traditional way of decorating paper and can look most effective, particularly if the shapes are applied as a border.

Materials
Fabric
Fabric inks
Stencil
Paper
Large potato
Craft knife
Powder or poster paints
PVA glue

STENCILLING
ON FABRIC

1 *Prepare your fabric by washing to remove any grease or surface finishing, then iron it out flat. Trace the pattern to be stencilled and cut it out of stencil card following the instructions on page 16.*

2 *If you are applying different colours to different areas of the design you will need to mask out the sections as you work to avoid getting paint where it is not wanted. Here the areas that are to be painted green are covered with masking tape while the red paint is applied with a stencil brush.*

3 *When the red areas are dry mask them out so that the green paint can be applied.*

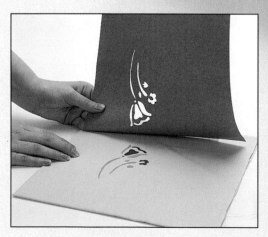

4 *Remove the stencil carefully. Most fabric dyes are fixed onto the fabric with a hot iron. Follow the instructions on the pot for the temperature of the iron and length of application. Allow the paints to dry thoroughly before fixing them.*

POTATO PRINTING
ON PAPER

1 *Choose a firm potato and slice it in half. Draw a simple shape onto a piece of card, cut it out and then anchor it to the potato with a pin.*

2 *Holding the potato firmly, cut down around the shape using a sharp knife. Slice the flesh away right up to the edge of the design so that the shape stands proud of the potato. This shape must have clear, defined edges so trim it if necessary.*

3 *Apply paint to the surface of the shape. Use water-based paints mixed with PVA glue to give more body and make the paint water-resistant. Press the cut potato firmly onto the printing surface. Each paint application should last for two prints, slightly fading on the second.*

SEWING

Tablecloths, napkins and placemats sewn in your own choice of fabric always give an individual look to the table. For a neat finish mitre the corners using a sewing machine or sew by hand.

    If you are making a padded placemat (see page 54) and using the mitre as a decorative feature, sew braid along the hem line to catch the hem and disguise it in one sewing step.

Materials
Fabric
Scissors
Needle
Thread

MITRED CORNERS
1 *Fold the corner of the material across at right angles so that there will be an even turn on each side. Iron in the crease.*

2 *Fold the cut edge in half, corner to corner, and sew along its length.*

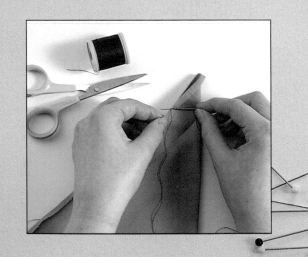

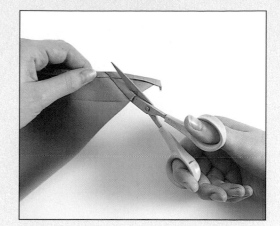

3 *Cut off the corner of the material along the crease.*

4 *Turn the corner inside out to form a mitre.*

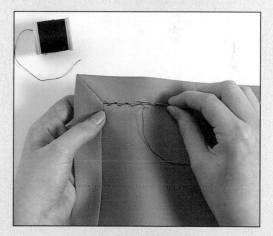

5 *Iron the mitre and hem the turning. You can sew a decorative line of stictching along the hem line on the right side of the fabric to enhance it.*

APPLIQUE MADE SIMPLE

An easy 'no sew' way of applying fabric appliqué is to use fusible bonding fabric. Shapes of contrasting material or printed patterns can be cut out and applied in this way to decorate tablecloths, napkins and other fabric items.

Materials
Main fabric
Fabric motif
Thick fabric paint writer
Fusible bonding fabric

1 *Wash the fabrics to remove the finishing which could interfere with the glueing process. If you have a shape or pattern already cut, as shown here, iron the bonding fabric onto it. (Alternatively, cut out a piece of bonding fabric in the shape of your required motif. Iron it glue side down on to the decorative fabric. Leave to cool, then cut out the motif and follow the instructions in step 3.)*

2 *Leave to cool, then cut off the excess bonding fabric around the shape.*

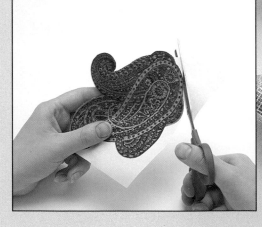

3 *Remove the backing paper and put the shape in position on the chosen background. Iron it down until it is firm.*

4 *Allow the material to cool. Seal the shape by piping thick fabric paint around the edge. When the paint has dried it will have trapped the raw edge and the raised outline will enhance the appliqué pattern.*

FRESH FLORAL SWAGS

Floral swags and wreaths are useful for decoration on the table and can be made with wet or dried arrangements. Try varying the scale from tiny wreaths to huge swags that run the length of the table. The bases can be bought, but it is much more fun to make your own.

Materials
Chicken wire
String
Sphagnum moss
Wire ties

WET SWAG BASE

1 Measure the length of your intended swag with a piece of string. Cut a piece of chicken wire about 30 cm (12 in) deep using the piece of string to measure the required length.

2 Tease out sphagnum moss and spread it in the middle along the length of the chicken wire.

3 Roll the chicken wire over and secure the ends with wire ties, lightly firming in the moss which will provide a reservoir for your flowers when they are added. Squeeze the roll into a sausage shape to use as the base of a swag.

4 For a wreath simply join the ends together using wire ties. Soak the wreath or swag in water. The easiest way is to plunge it in a bath for a while and drain it until it stops dripping. Wreath and swag bases can be stored like this indefinitely until needed, but remember to soak them before you use them.

WIRING FLOWERS

1 *Heavy blooms such as orchids and cymbidiums are easier to attach to swags if they are wired. Using florist's stub wires, make a hole through the top of the stem from the back, pushing the wire through.*

2 *Make a loop, twisting one end of the wire behind the stem.*

3 *Twist the two ends of the wire together. This gives support to the flower and provides an end to push into swags, wreaths and other arrangements.*

DRIED FLOWER ARRANGEMENTS

Dried flower arrangements in the form of miniature trees make attractive portable decorations that can be used time and time again. There are two easy methods of providing a firm base – by using a putty-like setting material or by buying a filled pot with oasis already cut to shape.

Materials
Base setting material and flowerpot
or oasis-filled pot
Stick
Oasis shape
Reindeer moss

USING SETTING MATERIAL

1 *Knead the 'putty', forming it into a ball in your hands.*

2 *Push a stick into the setting material and place it in a flowerpot. The 'putty' will set rock hard in about forty minutes.*

3 *Fill the pot to the top with reindeer moss to hide the rim. Continue to make the tree following steps 2-4 on page 27, and following the instructions on page 56.*

USING AN OASIS-FILLED POT

1 *Push a stick directly into a ready-bought oasis-filled pot.*

2 *Cut the stick to the required length, bearing in mind the final proportions of the tree you wish to make.*

3 *Place an oasis cone or ball on the stick, pushing it firmly down and making sure that it is positioned centrally.*

4 *Start building up background foliage using varieties such as sea lavender and oreganum. Continue to make the tree following the instructions on page 56.*

Atmosphere and Style

Creating the right atmosphere for a special meal makes an occasion memorable. The table setting, cloths, napkins and decorations are just as important as the food and drink, and the basis for success often rests on a careful choice of china, cutlery and glasses complemented by an appropriate decorative theme.

Entertaining can be intimidating, especially on a formal level, but it can also become an opportunity for creative fun. Give yourself plenty of time to work out the sort of atmosphere you want to create. Is it an event where tradition will dictate the style, such as a wedding, or can you break with the conventional and employ a more imaginative approach? A meal may be enhanced by a simple, relaxed style with soft candlelight or by classic, clean lines and plain strong colours. It is up to you to decide how to plan your table to delight and surprise your guests.

China

China is a term that applies to the whole range of crockery, from fine bone china or porcelain, through earthenware fired for different effects, to stoneware which produces a heavy rustic-looking pottery.

With such a huge variety of styles, patterns and quality, it is important to think carefully about your exact requirements before buying. The most sensible choice is probably to buy a good quality traditional set, particularly if you are going to be doing a lot of formal entertaining as it will last well and always look good.

Be sure to check all the details before deciding. If you are adding pieces gradually, is the range likely to be in production for some time? Is the pattern one that you will continue to like? Is it dishwasher-proof? Is it really necessary to have the top grade if you are not going to entertain formally a lot?

Two sets are an ideal solution, one for best and one for casual entertaining. The middle range of china is quite broad, and at one end of the market the patterns copy porcelain types, so for a considerably lower price you can purchase a service that will pass all but the most knowledgeable examination.

There are some delightful earthenware sets that are original in design and at a low enough price to replace when you feel like a change. At the bottom end of the range you will find 'cheap and cheerful' highly decorated earthenware. This is easily chipped, but none the less looks great for informal and outdoor eating.

An interesting idea that looks good, yet is very practical, is to opt deliberately for different plates and patterns. Stick to a distinct style, monotone print or a colour theme such as blue and white. It is quite easy to pick up odd plates at antique markets and a table set with a variety of old plates can be very effective. Stained plates can easily be whitened with lemon juice or a dilute solution of bleach. Complete the effect by using antique tablecloths.

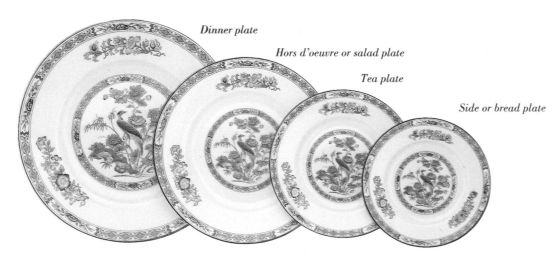

Dinner plate

Hors d'oeuvre or salad plate

Tea plate

Side or bread plate

The time-honoured way to serve tea is in a traditional bone china cup and saucer, with a silver teaspoon.

Tiny coffee cups or bonds are used to serve small quantities of strong black espresso coffee after a rich meal.

For coffee offered with milk or cream most people prefer to drink from a larger coffee can. Serve the milk and cream from separate small jugs.

How nice to offer overnight guests a late-night drink of hot chocolate in this elegant lustre-glazed china beaker!

Place settings

*There is a great variety of cutlery
to choose from and it is sensible to
buy two sets if you can, one for
formal entertaining and the other
for everyday use. Before buying,
try the pieces out for their balance
and grip – they should feel
comfortable to hold and use.*

*Silver and gold-plated sets of
cutlery are expensive but you can
add bits gradually. The top
quality companies have been
producing the same patterns for
years and they have become
traditional. Silver plate is a good
option but beware of really cheap
sets as the silver may be thin and
not so durable. Pewter and bronze
are attractive alternatives.*

*The lower price range of cutlery
offers stainless steel, with wooden,
plastic resin and china handles.
Choose a style and colour that will
suit your china and use – coloured
sets are fun but can limit your
table decoration.*

*This place setting shows
the cutlery set for a formal
five-course meal. Working
from the outside it shows
bread knife, soup spoon
and hors d'oeuvre fork,
fish knife and fork, dinner
knife and fork, and
dessert spoon and fork*

*An informal family place
setting showing bread
knife, soup spoon, and
dinner knife and fork. If
dessert is to be served the
dessert spoon and fork are
usually laid above the
plate, as shown in the
photograph on the left.*

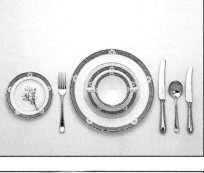

*If a starter is to be served
a small spoon may be
used. This is often brought
to the table with the
starter or may be laid on
a small plate as shown
here.*

*In the USA the bread
plate and knife may be
laid above the main
setting. The cutlery laid
shows soup spoon, fish
knife and fork, dinner
knife and fork, and salad
fork and cheese knife. The
dessert spoon and fork are
brought in with the
dessert, which is the final
course.*

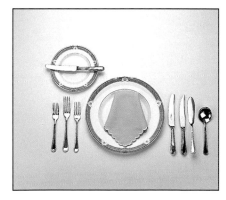

Glassware

In the past entertaining could mean a complete set of glasses numbering up to 15 or more different shapes. Today there are less rigid 'rules' on entertaining and an average social occasion at home probably only needs a tumbler and a decent-sized wine glass. For more formal occasions a generally accepted range of glasses is used.

The glasses you are likely to use include: **Sherry glass** *– a small capacity glass with a tulip or copita shape;* **Red wine glass** *– a wine glass with a shortish stem so that you can cup your hands around the bowl to warm the wine. A glass with a slightly narrower mouth is for more full-bodied wines to retain their aroma;* **White wine glass** *– a wine glass with a longish stem. White wine is usually served chilled and the stem keeps the hand away from the bowl of the glass;* **Champagne flute** *– a tall glass used for all sparkling wines to keep the bubbles in;* **Port and liqueur glass** *– similar but shorter than a sherry glass;* **Brandy glass** *– a balloon-shaped glass that you can cup your hand around to warm the drink. The large bowl of the glass captures the aroma.*

Other shapes that are commonly used are the **whisky tumbler**, *a straight-sided short glass. Neat spirits are usually served in conical-shaped glasses, but if a mixer is added then the drink is served in a whisky tumbler. In the USA* **'highball'** *glasses are used, as the high sides keep the bubbles in.* **Beer glasses** *are commonly a tankard or large goblet when serving formally, but a tall* **lager glass** *is acceptable now at home functions.*

If you are not serving wine from the bottle you can use a carafe or wine decanter. An open-topped carafe allows young red wines to breathe and oxidise in the air to improve their flavour. Serve older mature red wines from a stoppered decanter to prevent their bouquet or aroma from escaping. A wine cooler is useful for white wine to keep it chilled, and a nice luxury for champagne is to keep it in an ice bucket.

The quality of glass itself varies from high-grade cut lead crystal to recycled 'flawed' soda glass and the style you use depends on your personal taste.

Tablecloths and napkins

For formal occasions at home you need a good tablecloth. If you are buying one, take the measurements of your table with you to the shop. The cloth should hang approximately halfway to the floor, but can be longer for a more draped effect. Beware, though, of chair legs catching in the folds if it is too long.

Before buying, run through in your mind how many times you might have to launder and iron a beautiful piece of Irish linen, and if it seems too much then opt for a more serviceable cloth of polyester and cotton mix. One of the arts of entertaining is to be calm and relaxed in front of your guests, not to be on the edge of your chair when someone spills red wine on the tablecloth!

Tablecloths are very simple to make using extra wide sheeting that is available in a range of colours. A quick hemming job is all that is needed to produce several large cloths that can be dressed with lace or decorated in numerous attractive ways for grand occasions.

As with tablecloths, traditional napkins are of starched white linen. They are also large and with their generous proportions many beautiful designs can be folded. A number of classic napkin folds are demonstrated on pages 46–49.

Formal Entertaining

We often think of formal entertaining as requiring antique linen cloths set with fine china and crystal – yet an air of elegance and grandeur can be achieved with a minimum of expense. The secret of creating an imaginative formal atmosphere is to keep the decorations simple with a feeling of space.

By tradition white cloths are used on formal occasions, but with today's relaxed rules of etiquette many occasions can be enhanced by using coloured cloths, with similar colours carried through to the table's decorative details. A wedding table draped in soft pastels, with flowers and candles to match, can look delightful. A midnight blue cloth strewn with gold and silver stars can add a special atmosphere.

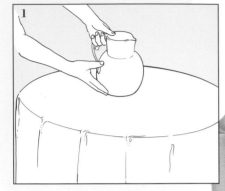

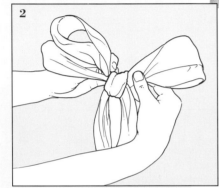

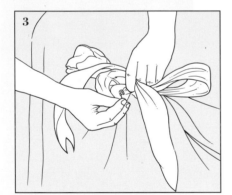

SWAGGED TOP CLOTH

1 *Choose two tablecloths and put the smaller one over a floor-length undercloth. Place a weight on the top cloth to stop it slipping while you work.*

2 *Make two large bows using two different coloured pieces of wired florist's ribbon. Cut the ends into a decorative 'V' shape.*

3 *Gather up the cloth in swags, catching the folds at the top with a stitch or a saftey pin. Attach the bows to the tops of the swags.*

▲ *A swagged cloth tied with bows in a colour scheme of soft pink and grey gives an unmistakable air of romance to any occasion. This easy-to-do look is equally effective on round, oval or four-sided tables.*

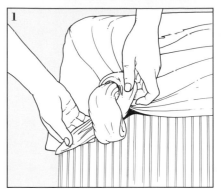

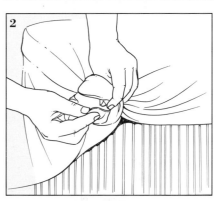

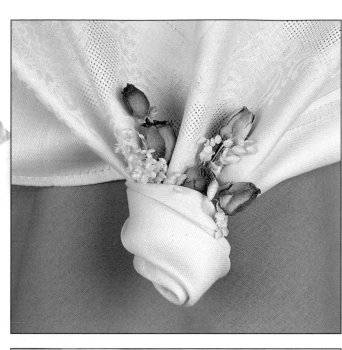

TURKISH KNOTS

1 *Gather up the corner of the top cloth and tie a knot in the cloth itself.*
2 *Tuck the end in and decorate the knot by tucking dried rosebuds and grasses into the fold.*

▲ *An undercloth with a decorative top cloth is a sure way of providing a simple dressed effect. Here, plain-coloured cloths are used and the top ones tied in stylish bows or Turkish knots.*

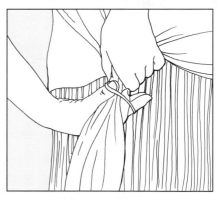

CORNER BOWS

Pull the corner of the cloth into a point and secure it with an elastic band. Hide the elastic band with a bow.

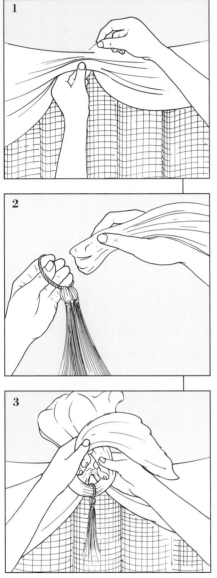

TUMBLING FOLDS

1 *Place a black and white checked undercloth on the table. Over this place a plain white cloth. Gather the top cloth to create swags.*

2 *Trail a length of net down the centre of the table. Bunch the fabric at each end and thread it through the loop of a tassel.*

3 *Tie the fabric around into a knot and leave the tassel to hang. Pin in place.*

▲ *This decoration is a simple swathe of organza placed around a fruit dish. The fabric is stencilled in a pastel green to complement the grapes, but brighter colours can be used for more exotic centrepieces.*

◀ *A dramatic undercloth and plain top cloth are a perfect foil to flocked net arranged along the length of the table. The gold tassel and underplates provide a continuous colour theme. Vary this effect by using tones of one colour to suit any table setting.*

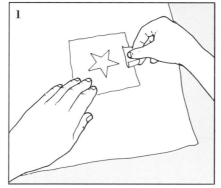

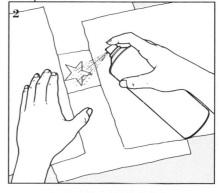

ORGANZA SWIRL

1 *Trace the star template on page 106 onto stencil card and cut out a stencil following the instructions on page 16. Cut a piece of organza long enough to loosely encircle your vase or bowl centrepiece. Place the fabric on a clean scrap piece of card and position the stencil on the fabric with masking tape.*

2 *Mask off the surrounding area of the fabric with clean scrap paper. Paint the star area using fabric spray paint. Leave to dry for about five minutes, then remove the scrap paper and stencil. Reposition the stencil on another part of the fabric and repeat the process until the all-over pattern is complete.*

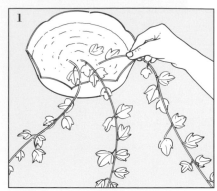

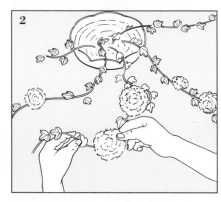

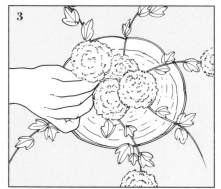

IVY TRAIL

1 *Fill a dish with water and place cut ends of trailing ivy in it. Arrange the ivy attractively on the table around the glassware and other items.*

2 *Trim the stems from the flowers. Position the flowerheads at intervals along the ivy trails, wiring them if necessary.*

3 *Add flowerheads to the dish to cover the cut ends of the ivy. Fill any gaps with short sprigs of ivy.*

LACE RUNNER

1 *Hem a piece of cotton fabric into a rectangle. Measure the outside edge, add half its length and cut the lace to this measurement. Starting at a corner, pin the lace to the fabric, allowing 1.25 cm (¹/₂ in) overlap so that some of the base material shows through. At intervals pull some of the lace together to create soft gathers; do this at the corners too. Sew the lace onto the material.*

2 *For the decorative bows cut 20 cm (8 in) lengths of lace ribbon. Fold the two ends together, pinching them into a central gather.*

3 *Sew the centre pieces firmly together to form a bow. Wind a thin piece of ribbon around the centre of the bow and stitch it at the back. Stitch the bows to the runner.*

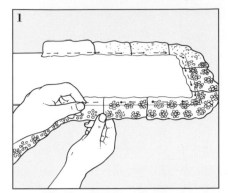

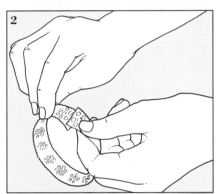

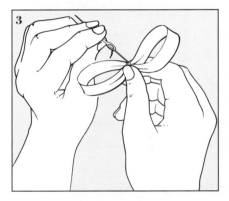

◀ *For a formal party or a wedding you may have to do with plain cloths supplied by a caterer, but a simple decorative trail of ivy and flowers can transform the table into something more special. Small-leaved varieties of ivy are the most suitable to use.*

▲ *This lace table runner makes a pretty addition to a plain table setting, especially if the background material matches or co-ordinates with the colours in the background cloth.*

PIERROT'S CAP

1 *Fold the napkin in half lengthwise from edge to edge.*
2 *Fold the bottom right-hand corner up and over towards the top to form the beginning of a cone shape.*
3 *Roll into a cone and turn the bottom up to form the brim of the cap.*

Pages 46–49 show some ideas for napkin folds. For best results you need napkins measuring at least 40 cm (15 in) square, preferably starched. Have a few spares lined up to practise with and give yourself plenty of time.

▲ *The pierrot's cap is a reminder of the traditional pantomime character's hat and adds a light-hearted touch of fun to a formal table.*

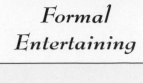

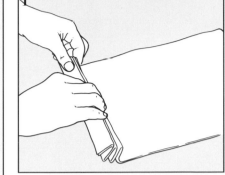

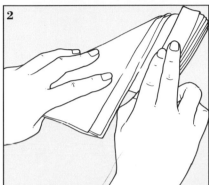

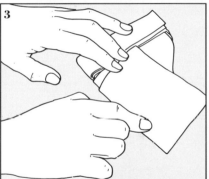

▲ A napkin folded in a fan can be used in a number of ways – placed on a plate or above the setting. The folds will retain their shape better if you use well-starched napkins. For a fan in a glass simply fold a napkin concertina fashion along its whole length, then fold it in half and place it in a wine glass.

CONCERTINA FAN

1 Fold the napkin in half lengthwise from edge to edge. Start making concertina folds from one of the short ends to just past the middle of the napkin.
2 Fold the concertina lengthwise, with the folds on the outside. Hold the folds together with one hand, and fold down the rest of the napkin diagonally.
3 Turn the bottom flap underneath to form a support for the napkin. Let the folds open out.

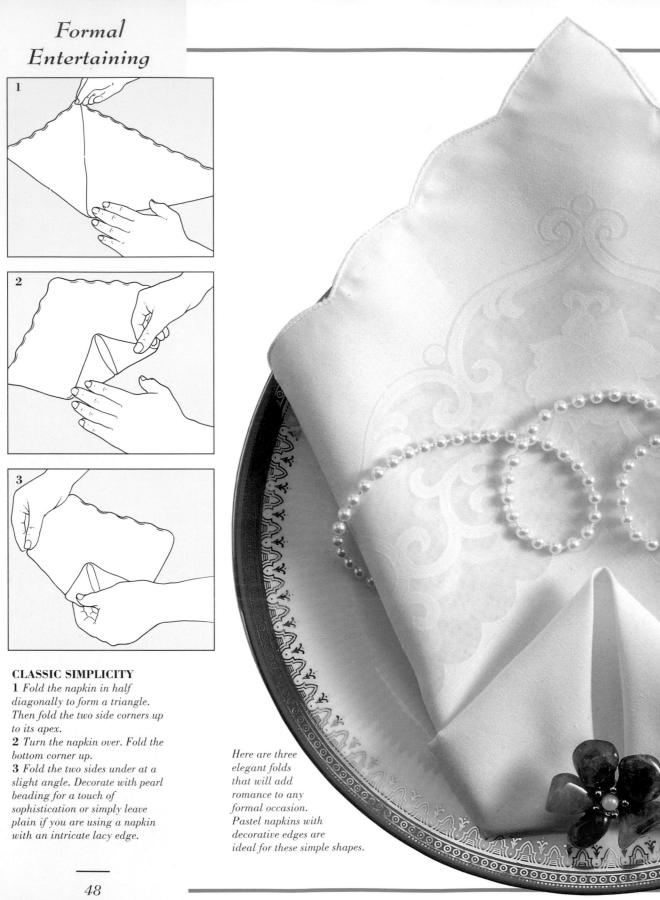

CLASSIC SIMPLICITY

1 *Fold the napkin in half diagonally to form a triangle. Then fold the two side corners up to its apex.*

2 *Turn the napkin over. Fold the bottom corner up.*

3 *Fold the two sides under at a slight angle. Decorate with pearl beading for a touch of sophistication or simply leave plain if you are using a napkin with an intricate lacy edge.*

Here are three elegant folds that will add romance to any formal occasion. Pastel napkins with decorative edges are ideal for these simple shapes.

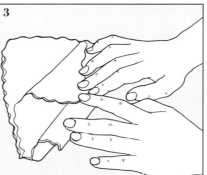

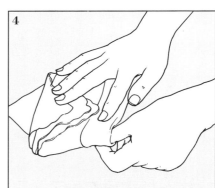

TIERED NAPKIN

1 *Fold the napkin into four, then diagonally into a triangle.*
2 *Place the napkin so that the four loose corners are on top. Fold the top layer over several times so that it forms a cuff along the bottom.*

3 *Turn the next layer down so that its point touches the cuff.*
4 *Fold down the other two layers in tiers. Fold the two sides behind and tuck one point into the flap of the other to hold it in place.*

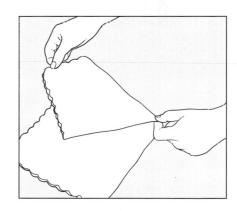

◀ *Use flowers or grasses to embellish these pretty napkins. A single red rose is the perfect decoration for a special Valentine evening.*

VALENTINE

Fold the napkin in half, then diagonally across so that the corner forms a point. Fold the other side to make a heart shape.

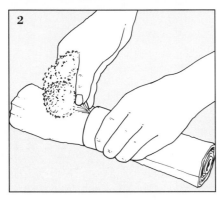

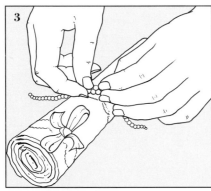

A rolled napkin provides a simple item to decorate. Here are some unusual ideas to try.

LACE DOILY

Wrap a circular paper doily around a rolled napkin. Secure it around the middle with wired ribbon tied in a bow. Trim stems of dried rosebuds to 2.5 cm (1 in) in length and insert them under the bow. Add pieces of bleached quaking grass.

SILVER RING AND FLOWERS

A crisp white linen napkin held in a gleaming silver ring looks extra special if some fresh flowers are tucked in. Trim the stems of two carnations and two sprigs of viburnum to 2.5–3.75 cm (1–1¹/₂ in) in length and insert one of each either side of the ring.

LACE TIES

Cut three pieces of lace trim. Tie one around each end of a napkin roll or slipstitch the ends together on the underside. Cover with organza ribbon tied in a bow. Tie the third length around the middle and secure it with a length of pearl bead trimming tied underneath.

PLAID BOW

Tie a tartan ribbon in a bow around the middle of a rolled napkin. Trim the ends in a fishtail. Cut sprigs of lavender about 7.5 cm (3 in) in length and tuck them either side under the ribbon.

IVY AND RIBBON

1 *Tie one end of a 60 cm (24 in) length of ribbon around one end of a rolled napkin. Twist the ribbon around and down the length of the napkin. Tie the ribbon end around the other end of the napkin.*

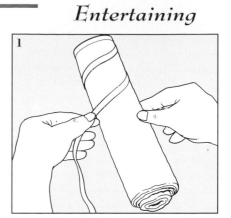

2 *Tuck ivy trails around the napkin, tucking the ends under the ribbon to secure them, making sure that they all go in the same direction.*

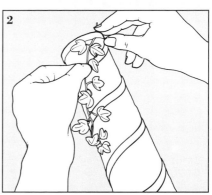

RIBBON TIE

1 *Cut a 60 cm (24 in) length of spotted ribbon. Tie it around a rolled napkin as you would a necktie.*

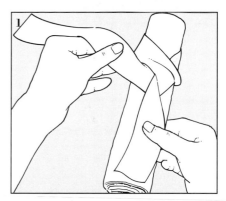

2 *Trim the ends of the ribbon in a 'V' shape by folding the ribbon down its length and cutting diagonally.*

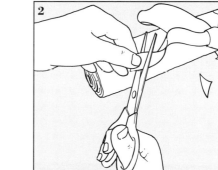

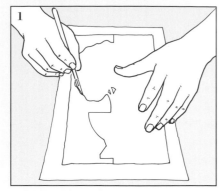

ORANGE TREE PLACECARD

1 *Use the template for the orange tree card on page 107. Using a piece of white card and a craft knife, cut around the tree shape. Score the card along the dotted line and fold back so that the tree will stand. Using the template on page 106, apply patterned paper to the card with spray glue to form the terracotta pot. Apply brown paper with spray glue to the tree trunk.*

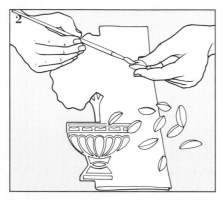

2 *Cut leaves out of green metallic paper using the template on page 107. Fold each leaf down the centre and apply glue on the back along the fold. Stick the leaves randomly over the tree. Apply glue to the backs of orange jewels or beads and stick them on to the tree. Write the guest's name on the card.*

NAPKIN HOLDER PLACECARD

1 *Using the template on page 109, cut the evening jacket out of black card. Make slits along the broken lines for the handkerchief and buttonhole. Glue buttons down the jacket front.*

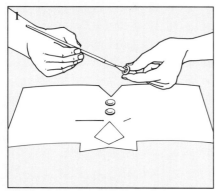

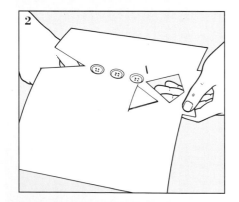

2 *Cut out the handkerchief name card from white card using the template on page 108. Write the guest's name on it and insert it into the slit from behind to show the name. Roll the jacket into a cylinder and fix the ends together with double-sided tape. Insert a sprig into the buttonhole. Insert a rolled white napkin into the 'jacket'.*

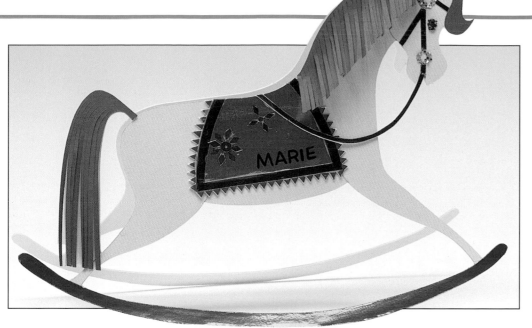

Formal place cards are fun to make. Choose a shape to match the theme of the occasion or make a different shape for each guest.

ROCKING HORSE PLACECARD

1 *Fold the card in half. Using the template on page 108, draw out the rocking horse making sure that the head and tail are on the fold. Cut round the shape with a craft knife.*

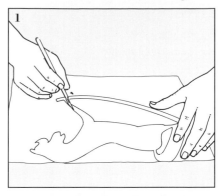

2 *Using the template on page 108, cut the saddle out of coloured paper and glue it to the horse. Cut a fringe, mane and tail out of brown paper and glue them to the horse. Write the name of the guest on the saddle and add any further decoration if you wish. If you want to decorate both sides of the horse cut out two saddles and make all decorations in duplicate.*

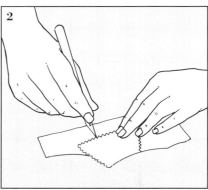

LEMON SLICE PLACECARD

1 *Using the template for a lemon slice on page 107, cut two circles out of pale yellow card for the front and back. Cut out the segments. Apply glue around the outer edge of one of the circles and stick down a circle of bright yellow tissue paper. Glue the front and back circles together, with the tissue paper between them.*

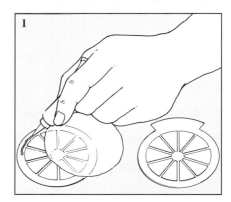

2 *When the glue is dry colour the outer edges of the circle with a yellow marker pen to represent the rind. Using a craft knife and steel rule, cut through one of the 'spokes' so that the lemon slice can fit on the side of a glass. Write the guest's name on the tag at the top. You could also make this placecard as an orange slice using pale orange card and orange tissue paper.*

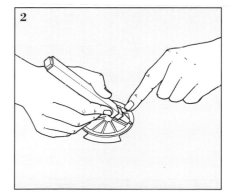

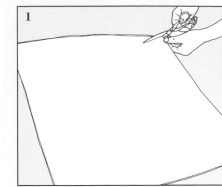

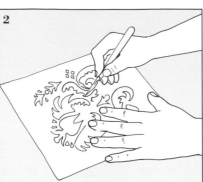

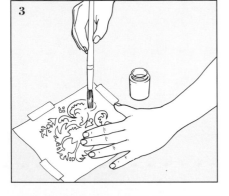

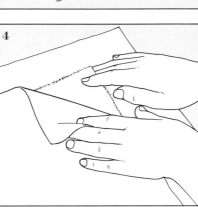

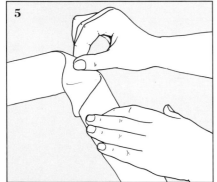

PRINTED DAMASK
PLACEMAT

1 Wash and iron the fabric as the printing inks will not adhere to it if it is greasy or has a finish on it. Cut out a rectangular piece of fabric for the size of mat that you want.

2 Trace the 'damask' template on page 110 onto stencil card and cut out a stencil following the instructions on page 16.

3 Using a sponge or a stencil brush apply fabric ink through the stencil to the top fabric, following the instructions on page 18. When dry, heat fix it with an iron, following the manufacturer's instructions.

4 Cut a piece of base material allowing for an overlap of 5 cm (2 in). Hem it around the edge. Cut a piece of wadding the same size. Place the top material face down, with the wadding layer on top and the base fabric on top of the wadding.

5 Mitre the corner of the base fabric following the instructions on page 20 and turning the edge over to form a border. Sew braid around the edge of the stencilled area to hold the top and base fabrics together.

▶ Damask linen is traditionally used in formal dining. This placemat is actually made from a cream cotton fabric that has been stencilled using white fabric ink to look like damask.

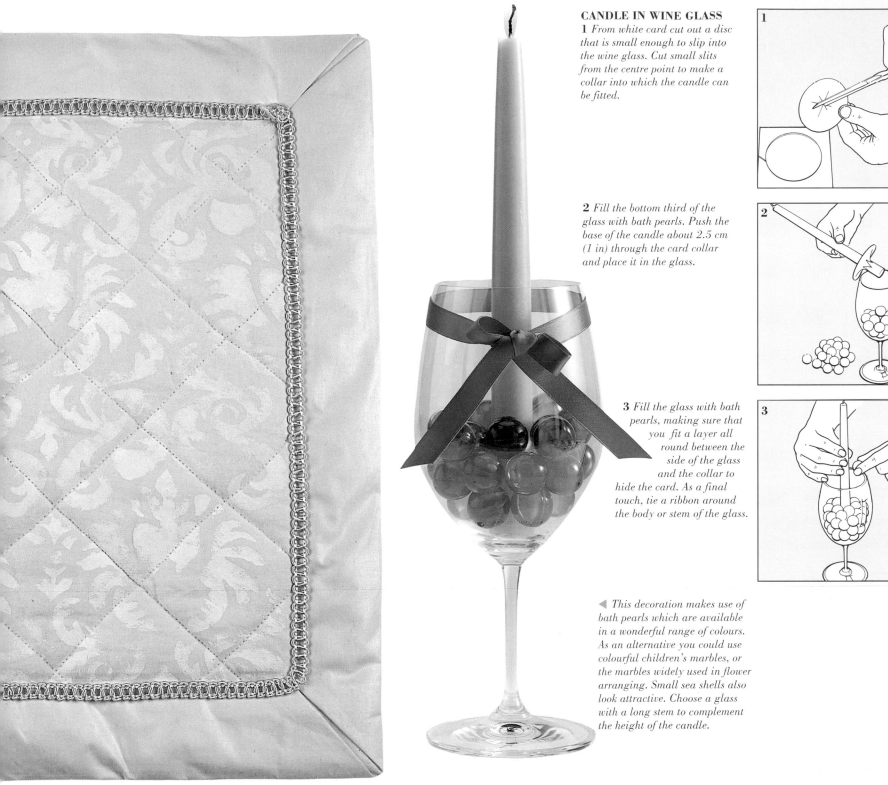

CANDLE IN WINE GLASS

1 *From white card cut out a disc that is small enough to slip into the wine glass. Cut small slits from the centre point to make a collar into which the candle can be fitted.*

2 *Fill the bottom third of the glass with bath pearls. Push the base of the candle about 2.5 cm (1 in) through the card collar and place it in the glass.*

3 *Fill the glass with bath pearls, making sure that you fit a layer all round between the side of the glass and the collar to hide the card. As a final touch, tie a ribbon around the body or stem of the glass.*

◀ *This decoration makes use of bath pearls which are available in a wonderful range of colours. As an alternative you could use colourful children's marbles, or the marbles widely used in flower arranging. Small sea shells also look attractive. Choose a glass with a long stem to complement the height of the candle.*

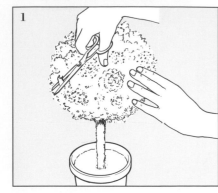

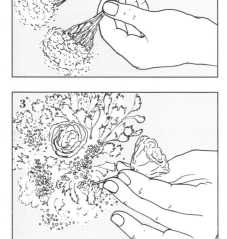

**DRIED POMPOM TREE
ARRANGEMENT**

1 *Set a twig firmly in a 13 cm
(5 in) flowerpot, using one of the
methods shown on pages 26–27.
Push a grey oasis ball measuring
9 cm (3½ in) in diameter firmly
onto the twig. Cover the ball
evenly with background foliage
of sea lavender, trimming the
foliage down to sprigs of about
6 cm (2½ in).*

2 *Continue to build up the
shape and fill in the gaps with
flowers, using broom bloom as a
background to the focal colour.
Break off the long stems.*

3 *Add the focal flowers of
rosebuds, orange carthamus and
carthamus buds. Finally, place
the flowerpot in a planter and
cover the top with clusters of
broom bloom and sea lavender.*

▶ *The neat shape of this
pompom tree made with
dried flowers and foliage
is enhanced by the use of
small flowers, making the
arrangement look densely
packed.*

◀ *This pompom tree made with fresh flowers and placed in a silver ice bucket would make an ideal decoration for a wedding reception, especially if the flowers are the same varieties as used for the bride's bouquet.*

FRESH FLORAL POMPOM TREE

1 *Soak a green oasis ball measuring 9 cm (3½ in) in water. Set a twig firmly in a 13 cm (5 in) flowerpot, using one of the methods shown on pages 26–27. Push the oasis ball firmly onto the twig. Cover it evenly with background foliage, using baby eucalyptus (round leaved), juvenile eucalyptus (pointed leaved) and senecio.*

2 *Place cream lily buds evenly around the ball, trimming the sprigs to about 6 cm (2½ in). Place cream freesias in the gaps.*

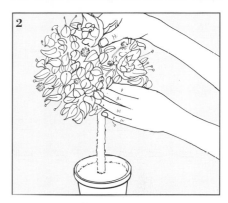

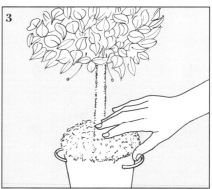

FLORAL CANDLE

Make matching candle arrangemants using fresh or dried flowers as appropriate. This simple arrangement features dried hydrangeas, but if you are using dried flowers to decorate a candle make sure you spray them with a flame-retardant substance.

3 *Add the feature flowers of cream and pink orchids, placing them randomly around the ball. Then add white gypsophila to soften the shape. Finally, place the pot in an ice bucket, so that the rims are level. Cover the top of the pot with wet reindeer moss.*

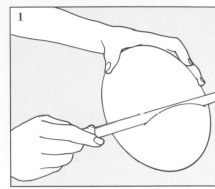

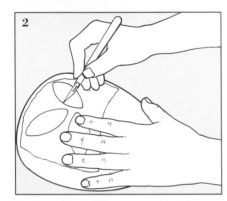

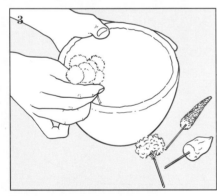

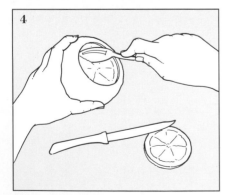

MELON AND CRUDITÉS CENTREPIECE

1 *Using a sharp knife, slice the top quarter to a third off a water melon. Level the bottom of the melon so that it will stand.*

2 *Trace the leaf design on page 110 onto paper and cut out the shapes to form a stencil. Attach the stencil to the side of the melon with masking tape. Score around the outline with a knife and cut away the outer skin of the melon to show the paler flesh.*

3 *Push vegetable pieces mounted on cocktail sticks into the soft flesh of the melon. Contrast the different shapes and colours of the crudités to create a pleasing arrangement. Vegetables to use include radishes, whole small chillies, spring onions, cauliflower florets, purple sprouting broccoli florets and baby sweetcorn.*

4 *To make attractive receptacles for accompanying dips, cut the top quarter from a grapefruit or small melon and scoop out all the flesh. Dry the inside of the 'container' with kitchen paper and fill with your chosen dip. Garnish by inserting a couple of crudités on cocktail sticks into the rim.*

RADISH ROSES

1 *Carefully trim the stalk and root end of the radishes.*

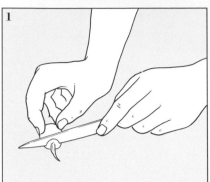

2 *With a sharp knife, cut the radishes in half from the root end, making sure that you do not cut right through. Similarly cut into quarters and then into eighths. Stand the radishes in ice-cold water overnight to open out.*

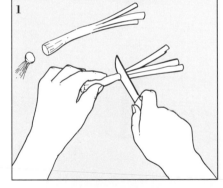

CHILLI AND SPRING ONION FLOWERS

1 *Use small chillies, or trim the pointed end from larger chillies. Trim the dark green stalks from the onions and the roots from the white part of them.*

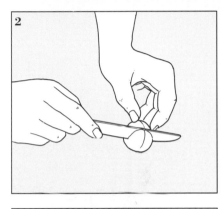

2 *Wearing gloves to protect your skin from the seeds, cut the chillies into narrow strips, finishing about 2.5 cm (1 in) short of the stalk end. Remove all visible seeds and pith. Cut the onions into narrow strips, finishing about 2.5 cm (1 in) from the white 'bulb' end. Leave the chillies and spring onions in ice-cold water overnight.*

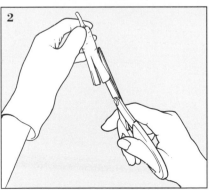

Country Style

A farmhouse kitchen table set for tea is
for many people the ideal informal
meal. You can easily recreate that
relaxed style in your own home
simply by adding a few country
touches to your table. Decorations
made from natural materials such
as salt dough, flowers and grasses
can evoke an atmosphere of harvest,
plenty and healthy living.

For a fresh look, nothing is more
delightful than a jug of cottage or garden
flowers. The secret is to mass them together
to make the most of their special quality. During
the autumn months dried leaves and berries can be
used for arrangements. Aim for a good variety of
colours and enhance them by wiping the leaves
gently with a slightly oiled cloth. Scatter leaves
casually over a tablecloth or pile them in a basket
for an unusual centrepiece.

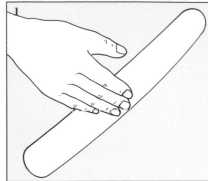

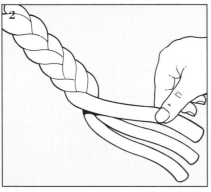

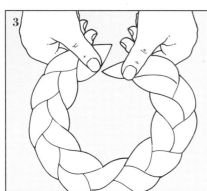

SALT DOUGH WREATH

1 *Make the salt dough following the recipe on page 12. Cut off a handful of dough and place it to one side. This will be used later to fashion roses and leaves to decorate the wreath. Roll out the rest of the dough into a sausage shape about 45 cm (18 in) long.*

2 *Cut the rolled dough into three equal pieces, then roll each of these into sausage shapes about 45 cm (18 in) long. Plait them together.*

3 *Cut the ends of the plait at an angle. Turn the plait into a wreath by bending it into a circle. Push the ends together firmly, sticking them together with flour and water paste. Add decorative details if you wish (see pages 63 and 65) before baking, painting and varnishing.*

SALT DOUGH ROSES

1 *To make each rose roll a small piece of dough about 1cm (¹/2 in) in diameter between your fingers. Then flatten the ball of dough between your thumb and first finger until you have a 'petal' just larger than your thumbnail.*

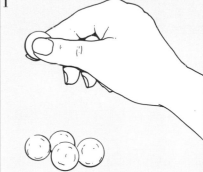

2 *Roll the petal into a tube to form a bud. Make another petal and press it against the bud. Add more petals to the outside of the rosebud until the rose is the size you want.*

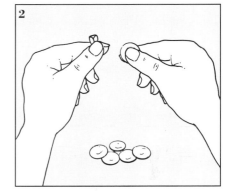

◄ *This salt dough wreath immediately adds a country feel to any table. It can be left in a simple traditional plait or decorated with smaller pieces such as flowers, buds and leaves. Roses add colour and interest, but a plain wreath decorated with ears of wheat would also look attractive.*

3 *Squeeze the lower edges of the petals together and cut off the excess. Brush flour and water paste onto the cut base and push the roses into the wreath.*

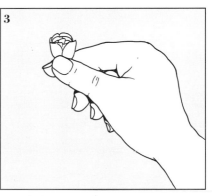

4 *Roll some dough out flat and cut out leaf shapes to go with the roses. For final detail make some tiny pear-shaped rose hips, indenting them at one end with a knife blade. Finally, cook the dough in an oven at medium temperature until hard. Colour the decorations with felt tip pens or paints. Varnish the wreath for a gloss finish to seal the dough.*

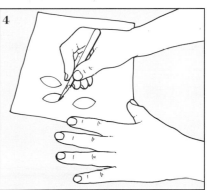

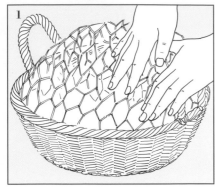

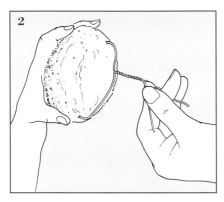

BREAD ROLLS
CENTREPIECE

1 *Buy an assortment of bread rolls or make your own from salt dough following the recipe on page 12. Leave the rolls to dry out or heat them in an oven, then varnish them with wood varnish. When they are dry pack out the base of a suitable basket with chicken wire. Mould the wire into a dome. Attach it with wire ties to the basket rim.*

2 *Use approx. 20 cm (8 in) lengths of malleable wire (garden wire is ideal) or florist's stub wires to pierce the rolls so that they can be attached to the basket. Push the wires through the sides of the rolls and twist the ends together. Secure them to the chicken-wire base. Check that the overall shape is even. Place some rolls over the basket rim to break the line visually.*

3 *When all the rolls are in place fill the gaps between with grasses and wheat ears, shortening their long stems and adding them in bunches. A few daisy heads or single spray chrysanthemums can also add a pretty touch.*

▶ *An unusual centrepiece made from assorted bread rolls would grace the table for an informal lunch or evening supper party. Its secret lies in choosing a good variety of shapes and colours and in placing the more interesting seeded and plaited rolls in prominent positions.*

WHEATSHEAF PLACE MARKERS

1 *Make salt dough following the recipe on page 12. Take a small fist-size piece, flatten it out on a board and mould it to an oval shape that is slightly domed in the middle. Aim for an overall oval of about 7.5 cm (3 in). With a knife, cut away the surplus dough to make a wheatsheaf shape. Mark lines to represent wheat stalks.*

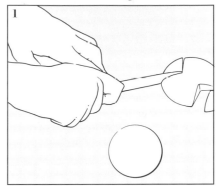

2 *Roll out the surplus scraps into a flattened ribbon and inscribe the name of the guest on it. Wrap this ribbon around the waist of the wheatsheaf. Impress wheat ears on to the sheaf with a toothpick or the end of a small knife blade. Bake and varnish when cool.*

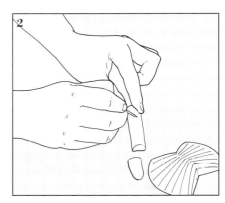

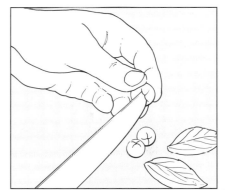

INDIVIDUAL SALT DOUGH WREATHS

Using smaller pieces of salt dough, make individual wreaths as described on page 62. Decorate these with small leaves, spacing the decoration evenly around the ring. Place berries on the leaves by adding small balls of dough, using flour and water as a glue. Make a small indentation on the bases of the berries with a ball point pen or a cross mark with a knife blade.

65

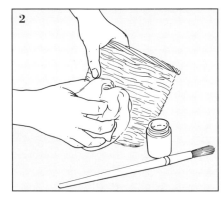

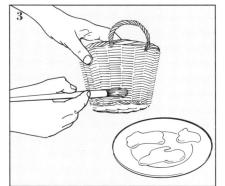

An attractive way of serving
breads, fruit and other items is
to use baskets as your serving
containers, lining them with
cloth napkins. These look good
at casual buffet parties, where
the baskets can be grouped
together to form part of the table
decorations. If you are using lots
of baskets with different
patterned cloths link them
together by keeping to the same
colour scheme.

SERVING BASKETS

1 *Choose a variety of baskets.*
2 *For an antique rustic finish use
acrylic-based paint. Almost
immediately rub it gently off the
wicker with a cotton rag.*
3 *Alternatively, mix pastel tones
with white silk-finish emulsion
paint to create a tinted limed effect.
Tip the paint out into jars and tint
them individually with powder
paints. Paint patches of
harmonising or contrasting colours.*

CHECKED NAPKINS

1 *Cut out a square of material that is large enough to fill the basket and fall over the rim.*

2 *Turn in a hem. Cut four pieces of ribbon about 30 cm (12 in) long, fold them in half and sew them in the middle to the corners of the napkin.*

3 *Place the cloth in the basket and pull it over the edges. Tie the ribbons onto the basket in bows.*

Country Style

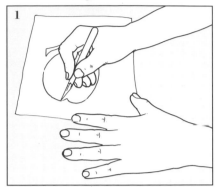

FRUIT PLACEMATS

1 *Using the templates on pages 111, 112 and 113 cut out stencils for the fruits following the instructions on page 16. Complete the fruit on one mat before working on the next. Mask out the leaves. Lightly sponge in the first layer of colour to the fruit. For a crisp outline use a stencil brush at the edge.*

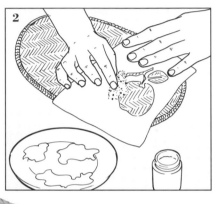

2 *While the paint is still slightly wet, sponge in a second colour on the fruit, merging the two together to give shading. Add a third colour in the same way if you wish. Finally, sponge in the leaves in two tones of green.*

▼ *Colour on cane or rush placemats will last quite a while if you use waterproof paint. For permanency use coloured inks as these will stain the mats.*

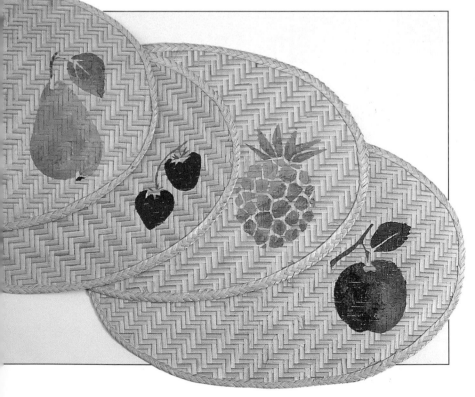

FISH PLACEMAT AND NAPKIN

1 *Cut out a rectangle of fabric measuring 45 cm (18 in) by 30 cm (12 in) and allowing an extra 1.25 cm (¹/2 in). Using the template on page 112, make a fish stencil. Stencil a row of fishes along the top and bottom of the fabric following the instructions on page 18. Heat fix the paint with an iron following the manufacturer's instructions.*

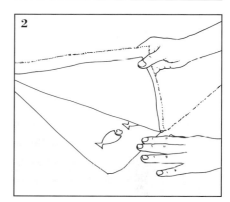

2 *Cut out a piece of polyester wadding the same size as the finished mat will be. Cut out a piece of backing fabric the same size. Place the stencilled fabric flat with the pattern uppermost. Place the base fabric on top and the wadding on top of that.*

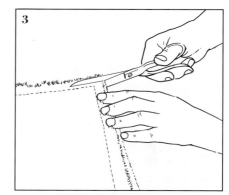

3 *Sew all the way round about 1.25 cm (¹/2 in) from the edge except for about 20 cm (8 in) in the middle. Make sure you stitch through all three layers. Trim the wadding close to the stitching and turn the placemat inside out so that the stencilled side is the right way round.*

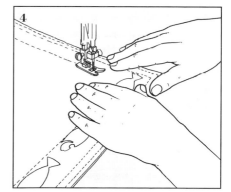

4 *Oversew the opening. Sew a double line of stitching as a border about 1.25 cm (¹/2 in) in all round the mat. Cut out a square of matching fabric and hem it to make a napkin. Stencil a fish in one corner.*

◄ *What better way to serve fish than at a table decorated with these attractive placemats with matching napkins?*

Country Style

DRIED FLOWER CENTREPIECE

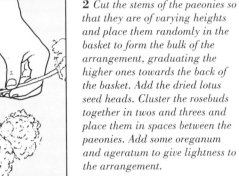

1 *Choose a low basket or bowl. Fill the bottom with grey oasis, cutting a block to shape. Place a little background foliage of copper beech around the edges of the basket to frame and define the overall shape.*

2 *Cut the stems of the paeonies so that they are of varying heights and place them randomly in the basket to form the bulk of the arrangement, graduating the higher ones towards the back of the basket. Add the dried lotus seed heads. Cluster the rosebuds together in twos and threes and place them in spaces between the paeonies. Add some oreganum and ageratum to give lightness to the arrangement.*

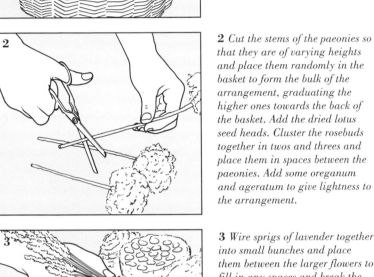

3 *Wire sprigs of lavender together into small bunches and place them between the larger flowers to fill in any spaces and break the heavy outline of the shape. Make sure the lavender sprigs are facing outwards to give movement to the arrangement.*

◀ A wicker basket provides an ideal container for dried flowers. Here, as with most flower arrangements, the contrast of colour and shape is important, and the large blown paeonies are set off by the lavender sprigs and small deep red rosebuds.

FRESH FLORAL WREATH

1 *Soak a green oasis wreath shape in water overnight. Dry the plastic base with a cloth and place the wreath in a good working position. Cut short sprigs of about 5 cm (2 in) long of foliage, including sweet box and waxflower, to give a varied background. Place the sprigs evenly all round the wreath, covering as much of the base as possible.*

2 *Cut the stems of the background flowers of white and peach spray carnations, including the buds, to match the height of the foliage. Place these evenly all round the wreath so that no large spaces are left.*

3 *Add the focal flowers of russet red spray chrysanthemums and button chrysanthemums, balancing the colours and shapes evenly around the wreath. Give the flowers a final light spray with water to keep them fresh.*

▶ *The rich autumnal colours of this wreath made with fresh flowers suggest the fullness of harvest time and the dark green foliage serves as an ideal foil to the russet red of the flowers.*

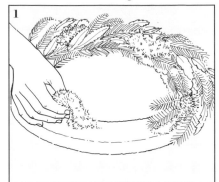

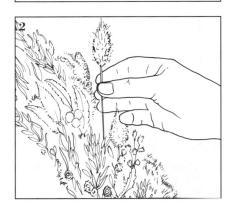

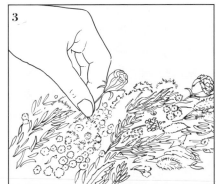

▲ *A variation on this dried flower wreath is to make it on a twig base and wind a ribbon around the circle. Wreaths made from dried flowers can last for a long time and if stored properly can be used again and again.*

DRIED FLOWER WREATH

1 *Cover a grey oasis wreath shape with black spruce, leatherleaf and coloured foliage. Work in one direction. Add reindeer moss at intervals to lighten the effect.*
2 *Add dried flowers and grasses, including lagerus, oreganum, ageratum and dill. Keep the arrangement evenly balanced in colour and shape.*
3 *Add rosebuds as features.*

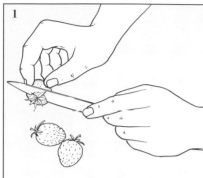

FLOATING FRUIT

1 Fill each compartment of an hors d'oeuvres dish with water. Remove the stalk ends from the strawberries and retain some of them for use later.

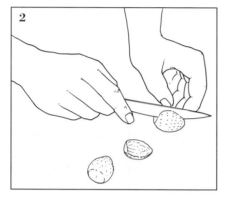

2 Cut the rounded sides from the strawberries and float them on water in one compartment of the dish. Add two or three green stalks for contrast.

3 Fill the other compartments of the dish with floating slices of kiwi fruit and kumquats. Lemon and lime slices or slices of cucumber also look effective.

▶ *For a simple small jug arrangement bunch herbs such as parsley and coriander together. Dill, with its fine fronds, gives a light contrast. Not only do you have an unusual green arrangement for the table but a useful way of keeping your herbs fresh.*

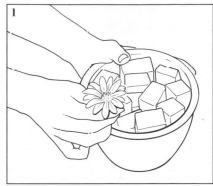

◄ *The vibrant colours of sliced fruits make an unusual and eye-catching centrepiece. This type of decoration is easy to prepare and requires only a few fruits of each type. Flower heads cut from their stems look attractive simply floated in a bowl, but it is important to choose the right contrast of colours. A blue glass bowl filled with white flower heads looks quite dramatic. For a more unusual effect, dye the water in a small bowl with cochineal and float a single yellow gerbera flower head. The trick is to choose light flowers with simple rounded shapes that will float well. Daisies, spray chrysanthemum heads and marigolds are ideal.*

DOME OF FLOWERS

1 *Fill a small bowl or shallow dish with pre-soaked wet florist's oasis. Shape the oasis into a dome with a craft knife. Trim the stems of the flower heads to about 2.5 cm (1 in) in length. Push the stem of a large flower into the centre of the dome.*

2 *Encircle the central flower with flowers of a different colour. Add a further ring of flowers of a contrasting colour.*

Country Style

COUNTRY BORDER TABLECLOTHS

1 *Using one of the templates on page 112 and 113, cut the stencil out following the instructions on page 16.*
2 *Check the spacing on your cloth. Measure the patterns so that they fit around the edges and corners without overlapping.*
3 *Follow the instructions for stencilling on fabric using several colours on page 18.*

◀ *One of the pleasures of stencilling is deciding what colours to use. The oak leaf border has several colours and needs a plain white or cream background. The trailing flower design looks good on a coloured cloth and looks quite different if you change the colour of the main flower. Wash the tablecloth to remove any finish and iron it before you stencil.*

▲ *A hand-painted set of glasses with matching jug is the perfect way to serve soft drinks when entertaining out of doors on a summer's day. Make sure that the glasses and jug are clean and dry before painting. Blend the paints on a saucer to achieve the tones you wish.*

GLASS AND JUG SET
1 *Using a thin paintbrush, dab in pink petals about 2.5 cm (1 in) down from the rim of the glasses. Dab in pink petals around the rim and under the jug handle.*
2 *Dot small orange flecks on to the petals on the jug. Paint in black dots at the centre of the flowers on the glasses and black dots and stamens onto the jug.*
3 *Paint the leaves with single short brushstrokes.*

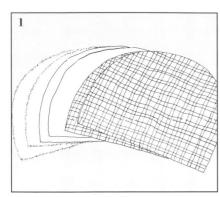

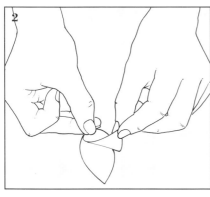

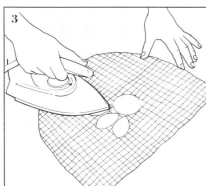

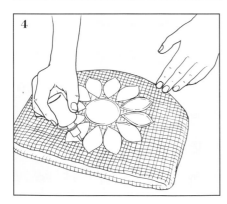

SUNFLOWER TEA COSY AND TRAY CLOTH

1 *Using the pattern on page 114, cut out two pieces of fabric for the outside of the cosy, adding on 2.5 cm (1 in) at the bottom for seam allowance. Cut two pieces of fabric for the lining and two pieces of wadding, using the same pattern.*

2 *Choose an appliqué motif. If using the sunflower on page 114, trace out 12 petals and and one centre circle on to bonding paper. Cut the shapes out and apply them to the fabric with an iron, following the instructions on page 22. Leave to cool, then cut out. Peel off the backing paper.*

3 *Follow the instructions on page 22 and iron the motif firmly on to the tea cosy. Check that the flower is in the centre and that there is room for all the petals. Place four petals first, then fill in the other eight.*

4 *Finally, pipe around the motif with thick raised fabric paint to seal the edges. Allow the paint to dry for 24 hours before you make up the tea cosy.*

5 *To make the cosy, place the two lining pieces together and the wadding either side. Pin, then sew all the way round, leaving the bottom open. Pin the two outside right sides together and sew around the curved edge. Allow a seam allowance of 6 mm (¹/4 in). Turn the outsides the right way.*

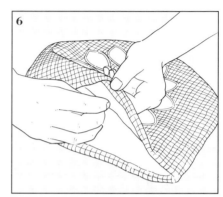

6 *Tuck the lining into the cosy and pin to hold in place. Turn the seam allowance to the inside of the cosy, and slip stich all around the bottom tucking the wadding in. For an additional finish you could pipe the seam edge or sew a braid along it.*

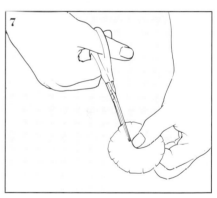

7 *To make the tray cloth, cut the gingham slightly larger than the tray. Cut the corners, mitre them as shown on page 20 and turn in a narrow hem. Alternatively, unravel the edge of the fabric to make a fringe. Apply a quadrant of the sunflower circle to one corner and four petals, following the above instructions for the tea cosy.*

◄ *This fresh gingham appliquéd tea cosy with matching tray cloth will help make a bright start to the day or revive your spirits with a well-earned 'cuppa' at tea time. Gingham napkins are an additional touch.*

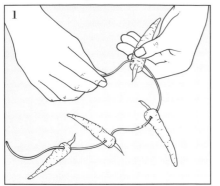

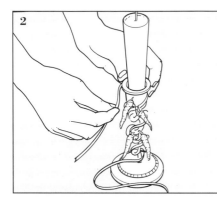

CHILLIES CANDLESTICK
1 *Thread dried chillies onto a length of fine wire. Wind the wire around the candlestick. Wash your hands thoroughly after handling the chillies, or wear gloves to protect your skin.*
2 *Wind a thin ribbon around the candlestick and tie it to secure, tucking in the ends.*

▶ *Try massing a number of candles and night lights of different sizes and colours for a stunning effect. Placing them in small terracotta flower pots in clusters around the table makes a delightful glow and you can decorate some of the pots with interesting paint effects.*

◀ *Single candlesticks can be decorated to echo the theme of the occasion or as a decorative item in their own right. Try using unusual items such as chillies or large beads. Another idea is to pick out colour themes by twining two contrasting ribbons around a candlestick. Tie them in a bow and cut the ends of the ribbon in a fishtail.*

TERRACOTTA CANDLES

1 *Paint the pots with a base colour of bright blue acrylic paint.*

2 *For a mottled effect sponge on dark blue paint in an even pattern all over the pot. When dry, sponge on gold paint.*

3 *Place a block of grey oasis in the base of the pot and push a candle into the centre so that it stands firmly. Cover the top of the pot with sphagnum moss.*

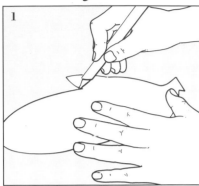

CORNCOB CLOTH

1 Take a large piece of scrap paper. Position a breadboard in the centre and draw a line around it. Trace the basic outline of the corncob template on page 115 and cut out ten cob shapes from scrap paper. Position the cobs around the circle in pairs. Draw around them with a bold felt-tipped pen.

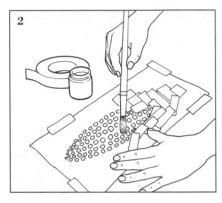

2 Trace the corncob onto stencil card following the instructions on page 16. Position a plain cotton tablecloth centrally over the corncob pattern on the large piece of scrap paper. Tape the stencil in position on the cloth. Mask out the leaf areas closest to the corn and apply deep yellow fabric paint to the corn area of the stencil with a stencil brush. Use a light stippling action, keeping the brush vertical.

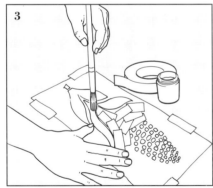

3 Remove the masking tape from the leaf areas and mask off the adjacent corn areas. Apply green fabric paint to the leaves and stalks. Complete one cob in each pair and allow the paint to dry before applying the second stencil. Follow the manufacturer's instructions for 'fixing' the paint, usually by ironing the cloth on the reverse.

▶ Picnics and meals in the garden can provide delightful memories of warm summers that stretch endlessly away with good food and company. By definition they tend to be informal occasions and the best china and glass are not necessary, so it is easy to add your own decorations and style. Choosing a harvest theme, such as corncobs and apples can set a relaxed mood from the outset.

CORNCOB GLASSES

1 *Tape the stencil to the outside of the glass. Using a fine paintbrush, apply deep yellow ceramic paint to the glass through each hole of the corncob in turn.*

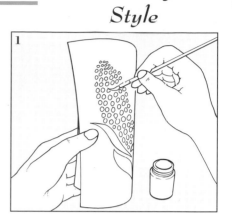

2 *Apply green ceramic paint to the leaf and stalk areas using upward strokes. Carefully remove the stencil from the glass.*

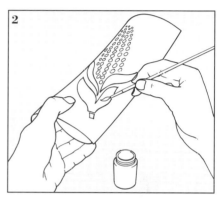

APPLE BREADBOARD

1 *Trace the apple template on page 115 onto stencil card and cut it out following the instructions on page 16. Tape the stencil to the board. Mask out the apple. Apply green stencil paint to the leaf and stalk areas with a stencil brush using a stippling action.*

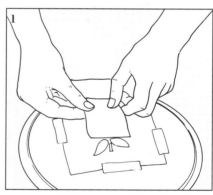

2 *When the paint is dry remove the masking tape from the apple and mask off the leaf and stalk areas. Apply red paint to the apple using the same method. When dry, add a few dabs of yellow paint to the centre of the apple. When all the paint is dry apply a thin coat of clear matt varnish to the board.*

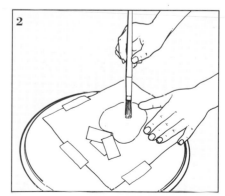

Special Occasions

Part of the joy in holding celebrations such as Christmas or family birthdays and anniversaries is in in trying to make the occasion extra special. Sometimes certain types of decoration are traditional and expected, but you can add your own individuality with careful planning and little effort. A special celebration need not be a costly affair and the time you spend in making one or two unusual items will reap its reward in the effect you create.

Many of the ideas presented here can be adapted for a variety of occasions. The Christmas crackers on page 89, for instance, could also be made in silver or gold foil for a Silver or Golden Wedding anniversary. Swags, shown on pages 92 and 94 are simple to make, and versatile in their effect – they can be made from dried flowers or evergreens for a Christmas gathering, and fresh flowers for a summer's evening party.

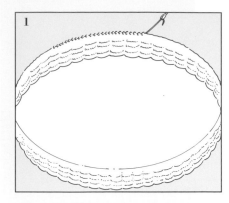

RIBBONS AND ROSETTES

1 *Measure the circumference of a circular tablecloth for the length of trim required and add a little extra to allow for overlap. Using lace trim with two finished edges, oversew the edges of the cloth and lace together back to back. Stitch so that the trim is flat to the cloth and catch the stitch lightly so that the lace will hang down flat without sticking out.*

2 *To make a ribbon rosette, hand sew a line of running stitches close to one edge of a length of ribbon. Pull the thread to gather the ribbon into a circle. Oversew the centre of the rosette on the reverse to secure it.*

3 *Make a second rosette in a contrasting colour of ribbon. Sew the two centres together at the back to create a double rosette. Sew the rosettes onto bows, pinning them onto the tablecloth at the top so that they hang down.*

▶ *A pretty idea for a wedding is to trim a cloth with a border of petticoat lace and embellish it with huge celebratory bows and rosettes.*

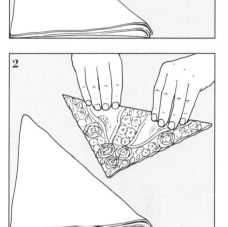

▲ *An effective and easy way to dress up a napkin is to present it in a lacy doily folder. For a Gold or Silver Wedding anniversary spray the doilies with gold or silver paint.*

▼ *A gold doily looks stunning used as an underplate decoration, especially if it complements gold edging on the china.*

DECORATIVE DOILIES
1 *Fold the napkin diagonally. Choose a square or round doily and fold this diagonally.*
2 *Make a second fold along the bottom of the doily about 1 cm (3/8 in) from the first. This will allow for the thickness of the napkin when it is inserted in its folder. Decorate with fresh flowers or a small trinket.*

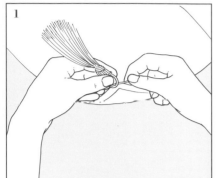

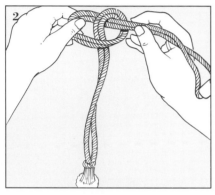

CORD AND TASSELS

1 *Cover the table with a cream or ivory lacy cloth. Add hemmed squares of fabric in co-ordinating colours to hang down in points. Sew a tassel to each point.*

2 *Tie the ends of double cords with tassels into large attractive knots. Pin them to the table at intervals so that the tassels hang down the sides.*

3 *Link the tassels with a loop of single cord pinned to each knot.*

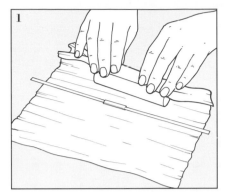

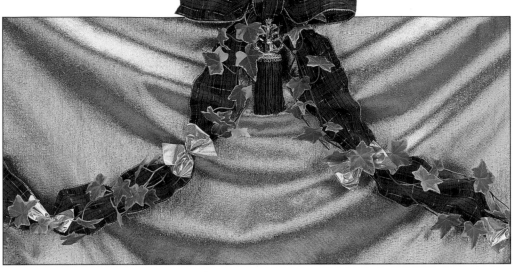

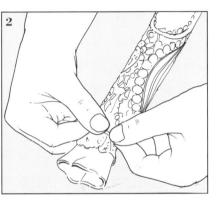

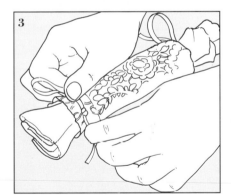

▲ *Another simple decoration for a plain cloth is to tie a decorative ribbon in a bow and pin it to the table to make swags. Pin a tassel to the bow, then pin smaller gold bows at intervals along the swags. Twine variegated ivy around the ribbon.*

◀ *Gold cord and tassels add a special touch to a festive table, linking colours and patterns together. This effect works best with slightly textured tablecloths in rich colours.*

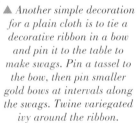

CHRISTMAS CRACKERS

1 *Tuck sweets, charms and mottoes into a small cardboard tube. Wrap the tube in crepe paper, with it overhanging the tube at each end.*
2 *Roll a doily around the tube. Bunch up the paper at each end, securing it with elastic bands.*
3 *Cover the elastic bands with glittery string or ribbon tied in a bow. Paste decorative shapes onto the cracker.*

CANDLE WREATH

1 Soak a green oasis wreath shape in water overnight. Dry it with a cloth. Push four plastic candle-holders into the wreath.
2 Cover the wreath with evergreen foliage, using sweet box and fir, overlapping the edges to hide the plastic base. If the wreath is only to last for a short time add green poinsettia leaves.
3 Place red poinsettia bracts around the wreath. Place red candles in the four holders.

▲ This Christmas candle wreath is decorated with poinsettia, but it would look equally effective decorated with holly and ivy. You could make a wreath like this for other special occasions and decorate it with seasonal flowers and pastel-coloured candles.

▼ *Ordinary fruits sprayed in metallic colours make a dramatic centrepiece when heaped together. You could use textured fruits as well as smooth-skinned ones, and include some nuts. The contrast of green leaves against gold and silver fruits enhances the arrangement.*

Always wear a mask when using car spray paint.

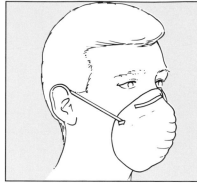

GOLD AND SILVER FRUITS

1 *Lay apples, pears and grapes out on newspaper and spray them with gold and silver car spray paint.*

2 *Line a suitable container – a silver cakestand or china bowl – with leaves or a doily.*

3 *Pile the fruit onto the dish. Arrange variegated ivy in the gaps between the fruits.* **NB Do not eat any painted fruit.**

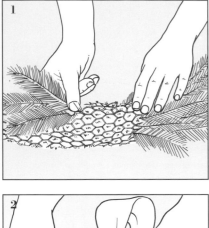

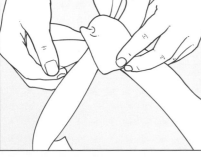

EVERGREEN SWAG

1 *Make a swag base following the instructions on page 24. Cover it with evergreen foliage such as yew or fir, tucking the stems in firmly and working outwards towards the ends.*
2 *Make two bows using gold-coloured florist's wired ribbon. Wire these onto the swag.*
3 *Wire red, gold, bronze and clear shiny Christmas tree balls evenly along the swag.*

DECORATIVE SHAPES

1 *Make salt dough following the instructions on page 12. Roll it out to about 75 mm (¹/4 in) thick. Cut out Christmas shapes with pastry or biscuit cutters. Pierce a hole at the top of each shape for hanging and at the bottom of the bell shapes to add a 'clapper'. Bake the shapes. Paint the pieces, then varnish them five times to give a high gloss finish.*

2 *Paint details on the bell shapes with gold paint. Hang the shapes on glitter thread, tying the knot just above the hole so that they will hang straight. Glue gold bows to the tops of the bells.*

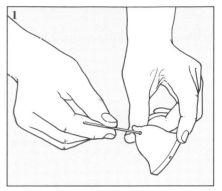

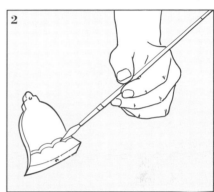

◀ *Bring a festive air to the buffet table by using Christmas baubles and bows to make this evergreen swag. Similar swags can be made for special birthday parties by choosing different colour schemes.*

3 *Push a pipecleaner into a bead. Cut the end about 1 cm (³/8 in) above the bead. Glue the end into the hole at the bottom of the bell.*

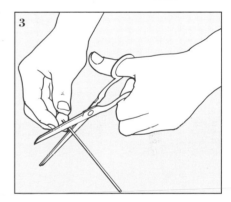

▲ *These painted salt dough decorations in gold, silver and scarlet look good hanging on an evergreen swag or simply on a bunch of twigs in a jug.*

EVENING BUFFET SWAG
*1 Make a moss sausage base
following the instructions on
page 24. Cover the swag base
with foliage, using eucalyptus,
senecio and asparagus fern.*
*2 Add the white chrysanthemums
and gypsophila.*
*3 Add the feature flowers of
purple and blue anemones and
freesias. Check that the
arrangement is balanced visually
by concentrating the feature
flowers towards the centre.*

▲ *A swag displaying fresh
flowers makes an attractive
decoration for the front of a
buffet table. Tuck in the stems of
the flowers so that they face
directionally. Make sure that the
flower heads tilt up slightly
towards the top of the swag so
that you can see them from eye
level when the swag is placed in
position on the side of the table.*

NAPKIN WITH CUTLERY

1 *Fold the napkin in four to make a square, with the open edges at the top right-hand corner. Take the corner of the top layer of the napkin and fold it to the bottom left-hand corner to make a crease.*

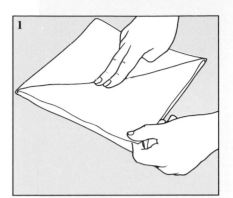

2 *Fold the top layer of the napkin under three times, making the third fold along the crease and leaving a diagonal pocket between the top two layers.*

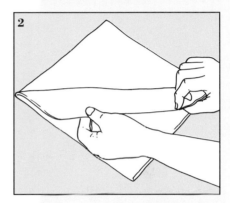

3 *Fold the second layer under twice in the same way. Tuck the edge of this second pocket into the first pocket.*

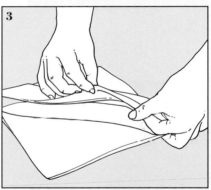

SUGARED ALMOND GIFTBAGS

Net twists of almonds are traditionally given at weddings and christenings, when they should contain one gold almond to bring luck. These giftbags also make pretty table decorations and can be taken home by guests at the end of an evening party. Cut two or three circles of net and place a lacy handkerchief on top of them. Put in the sugared almonds. Secure the handkerchief and net with an elastic band and tie a ribbon in a bow to hide it.

4 *Fold the left and right-hand sides of the square underneath. Place a knife, fork and spoon in the two pockets of the napkin.*

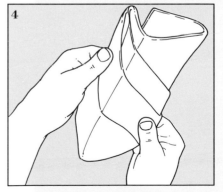

Children's Parties

Children's parties can be a nightmare for busy parents, but here are some ideas that are fun and easy to do. Many of them can be planned and carried out with the help of the children themselves. Along with bold, bright colours, decorative themes that cover every aspect of the party are popular and are a good way of helping children and adults alike to enter into the spirit of the occasion.

Again, planning a theme can be quite inexpensive. Large plain paper tablecloths are available in supermarkets and are ideal for stencilling, along with matching napkins, paper cups and plastic glasses. The theme can be continued into various other items for the party, such as small gift packages to take home afterwards (see page 102). Choose food to complement the theme, labelling it accordingly, and match drinking straws to the colour of drinks.

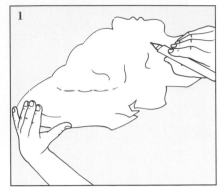

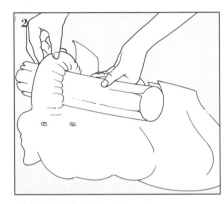

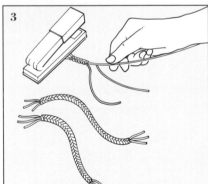

ELEPHANT PLACEMATS

1 *Cut the elephant out of grey card using the template on page 117. Draw the details in using a dark grey marker pen. Glue joggle eyes on in place using PVA glue. Glue on white card toenails and tusks .*

2 *Cut logs out of brown card and end pieces out of cream card. Glue the end pieces on to the logs. Draw on the details with brown marker pen. If you wish to add names paint them on at this stage using cream-coloured poster paint. Cut along the inside of the elephant's trunk with a craft knife and pass the log through from front to back.*

3 *Tie the ends of three different shades of grey wool in a knot and secure under a heavy object. Plait the wool almost to the other end. Tie it off with a piece of wool, leaving a tassel. Glue or tape the knotted end to the underside of the card at the back of the elephant.*

▶ *Children love theme parties, and a table setting featuring wild animals is a sure winner. It is quite easy to draw a variety of animals such as giraffes and monkeys by tracing basic shapes from magazines and books. The animals can be simple outlines and need not be drawn in great detail. The size of this elephant placemat is based on seating four around a 120 cm (48 in) diameter table top.*

LION CUPS

1 *Paint lion faces onto yellow paper cups with brown poster paint.*

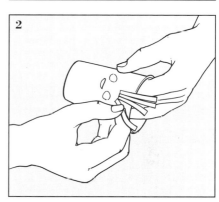

2 *Cut strips of orange tissue paper 37 mm (1½ in) long. Glue them around the face area to form a mane. If the mane is too long give it a trim when complete.*

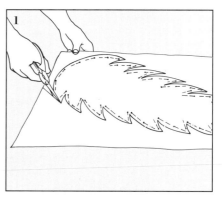

JUNGLE LEAVES

1 *Draw the leaf onto tracing paper following the template on pages 118–119. Cut it out and pin it to a piece of green felt that has been folded into four. Cut around the leaf. Cut out a circle of felt 25 cm (10 in) in diameter for the centre of the table.*

2 *Place the leaves on the tablecloth, radiating out from the centre following the guide on page 116. Place the circle of felt in the centre to hide the ends of the leaves. This can be used as a base on which to place a basket of fruit.*

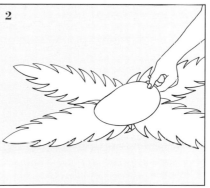

COUNTERS CUPS

Cut out 'counters' in the four primary colours and glue them to the paper cups with PVA glue. Use only one colour for each cup. Repeat the process with paper plates and paper napkins.

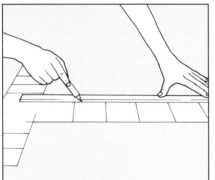

SNAKES AND LADDERS TABLECLOTH

Draw the ladders out into position on a piece of tracing paper following the guide on page 116. Then lay the tablecloth over the tracing and trace off the ladders using a ruler and a black fabric pen. For each ladder rule two parallel lines 47.5 cm (19 in) in length, 10 cm (4 in) apart. Rule rungs across at 6 cm (2½ in) intervals.

SNAKES

1 *Using the template on pages 118–119, cut the snakes out of card with a craft knife. Use coloured card to match the primary colours of the cups and plates.*

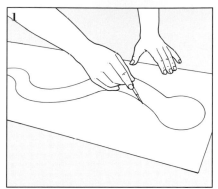

2 *Mark out a pattern on each snake. Using PVA glue, fix co-ordinating sequins to fill the pattern.*

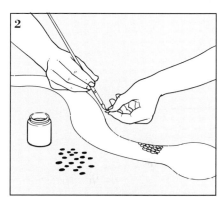

3 *Fix joggly eyes to each snake with PVA glue. Cut the snake's tongue from black card using the template on page 118 and glue it under the snake's head at the top.*

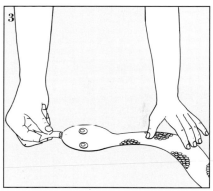

◀ *Games are an important part of children's parties and this one is designed around the popular board game of snakes and ladders. A simplified version of the game could be played after the meal by linking the snakes across the places to the ladders around the table. Supply the children with counters and roll a dice to count their moves up the ladders towards the prizes in the centre of the table. If the counter lands on a snake's head the player 'slides down' to the bottom of the ladder. The measurements here allow four ladders to fit on a 120 cm (48 in) table.*

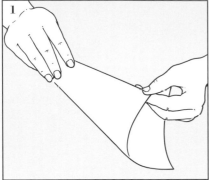

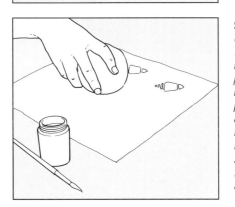

PIRATE FAVOUR

1 *Using the template on page 120, cut out a square of paper or thin card measuring 190 mm x 190 mm (7¹/2 in x 7¹/2 in). With a craft knife make slits where indicated on the template. Fold the card into a cone shape and fix it together with double-sided tape.*

2 *Using the template on page 121, cut out the eye, eye patch, nose and ears. Attach them with PVA glue inserting the ears into the slits. Fold the flap of the cone over. Glue several lengths of black wool to the lid to represent hair. Tie a knot in a spotted handkerchief or remnant and glue it on top of the hair using PVA glue. Glue a brass curtain ring onto the left ear.*

SEASHELL FAVOUR

Using the template on page 121 and following the instructions for potato printing on page 19, print the shell motif onto a piece of patterned paper. Leave to dry, then glue to a piece of metallic paper. When dry make a cone shape following Step 1 for the Pirate Favour. Fold the flap to form a lid, and fill with sweets.

▲ *Children like to find a small gift by their place at the table. Wrapped and jellied sweets are always popular and can be put into brightly coloured cones that follow the theme of the party. These individual 'favours' can then be taken home at the end of the afternoon.*

▲ This pirate's treasure chest filled with gold-covered chocolate coins makes an attractive centrepiece for a children's party. Individual chests can be made as prizes or take-home gifts.

TREASURE CHEST

1 *Following the template on page 122, cut the chest out of brown card.*

2 *Fold along the scored lines to make the chest shape. Fix double-sided tape to the tabs to secure the sides in place. Cut out the two end pieces of the lid and fix them on using double-sided tape, having scored around the tab 'teeth'.*

3 *Decorate the chest with gold paint or metallic paper.*

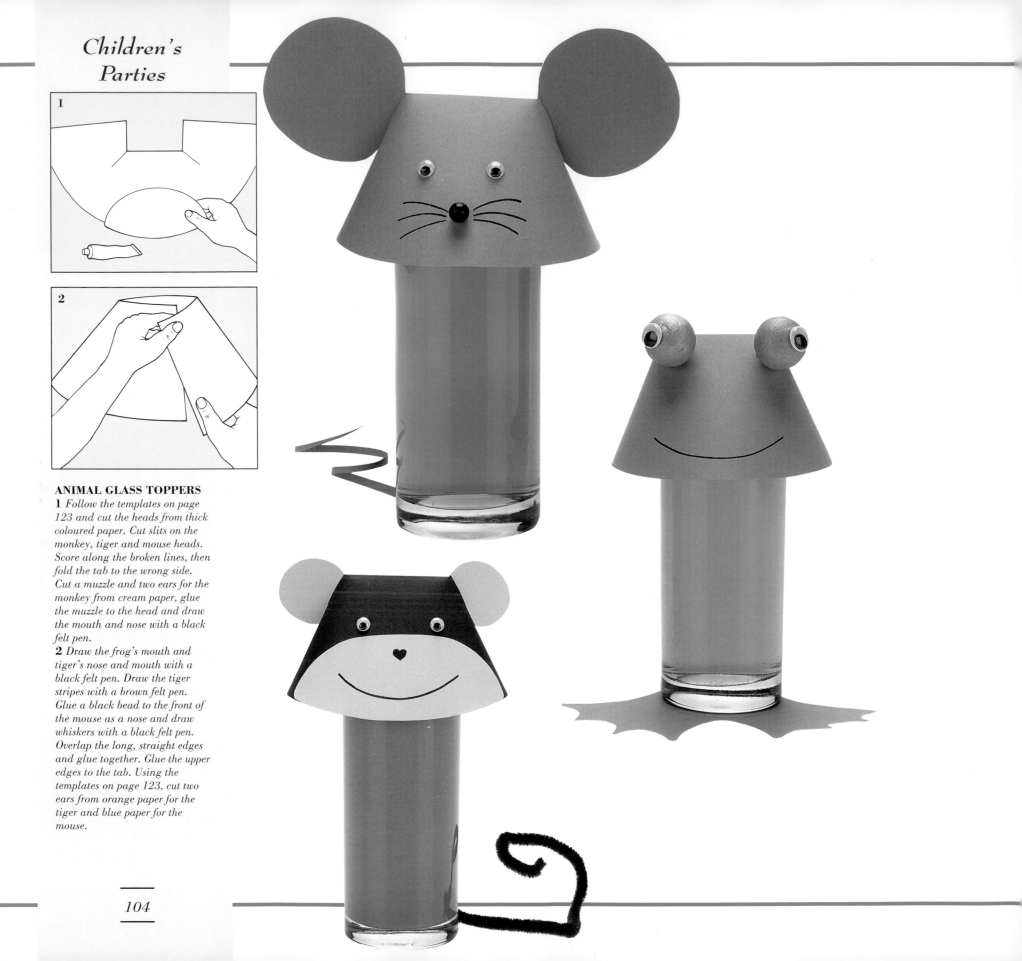

ANIMAL GLASS TOPPERS

1 *Follow the templates on page 123 and cut the heads from thick coloured paper. Cut slits on the monkey, tiger and mouse heads. Score along the broken lines, then fold the tab to the wrong side. Cut a muzzle and two ears for the monkey from cream paper, glue the muzzle to the head and draw the mouth and nose with a black felt pen.*

2 *Draw the frog's mouth and tiger's nose and mouth with a black felt pen. Draw the tiger stripes with a brown felt pen. Glue a black bead to the front of the mouse as a nose and draw whiskers with a black felt pen. Overlap the long, straight edges and glue together. Glue the upper edges to the tab. Using the templates on page 123, cut two ears from orange paper for the tiger and blue paper for the mouse.*

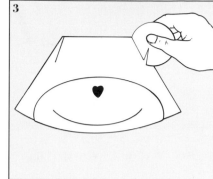

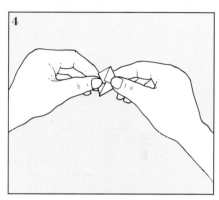

3 Cut slits in the ears and insert the narrow ends through the head slits. Paint two cotton pulp balls green and glue them to the top of the frog. Cut a coaster from thick green paper for the frog and thick yellow paper for the bird, using the templates on page 123. Stand the glasses on the coasters.
4 Score the beak along the broken lines, overlapping the tabs. Glue the tabs together, then glue the beak to the bird. Glue joggle eyes to all the creatures. Slip pipecleaner 'tails' under the monkey and tiger glasses. Cut a narrow strip of blue paper, pull it over a scissor blade to coil it and slip it under the mouse glass as a tail. Glue feathers to the bird and the back of its glass.

▲ These colourful animal characters are a fun way to bring drinks to life at a children's party. Make them in a variety of colours, matching them to the colour of the drinks you are serving.

Templates and Patterns

The following pages present the templates and patterns referred to in the table decorating projects.

The templates printed in blue are reduced in size. To enlarge, draw a grid of 1.4 cm (9/16 in) squares. Copy the design square by square using the lines as a guide. Alternatively, enlarge templates on a photocopier to 141% (or A4 enlarged to A3). To make a complete pattern for symmetrical shapes, place the pattern on a piece of folded paper matching the 'place to fold' line to the folded edge. Cut out and open the pattern out flat to use.

Remember, too, that it is fun to use your own shapes and designs, following the same principles. Trace out the basic outline from a magazine or book onto graph paper and enlarge or reduce it accordingly. Keep the shapes simple and enjoy using your imagination.

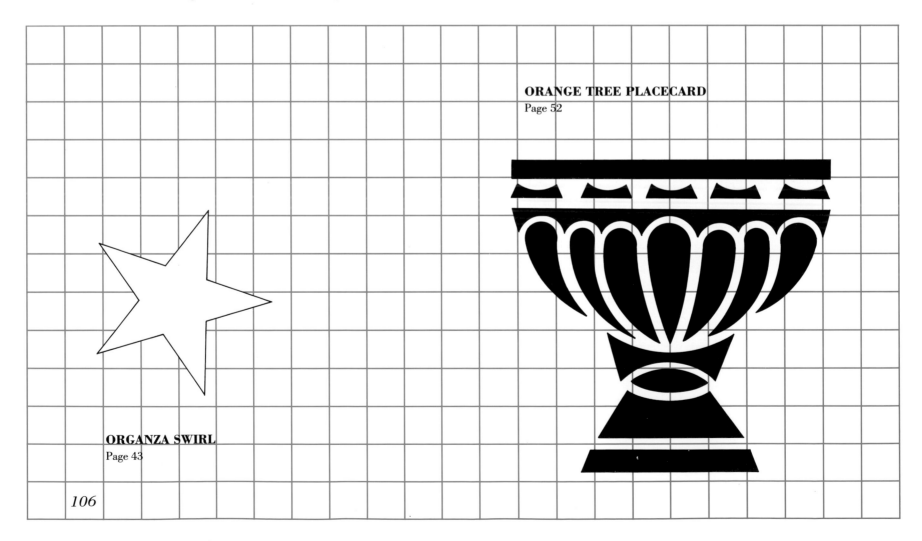

ORANGE TREE PLACECARD
Page 52

ORGANZA SWIRL
Page 43

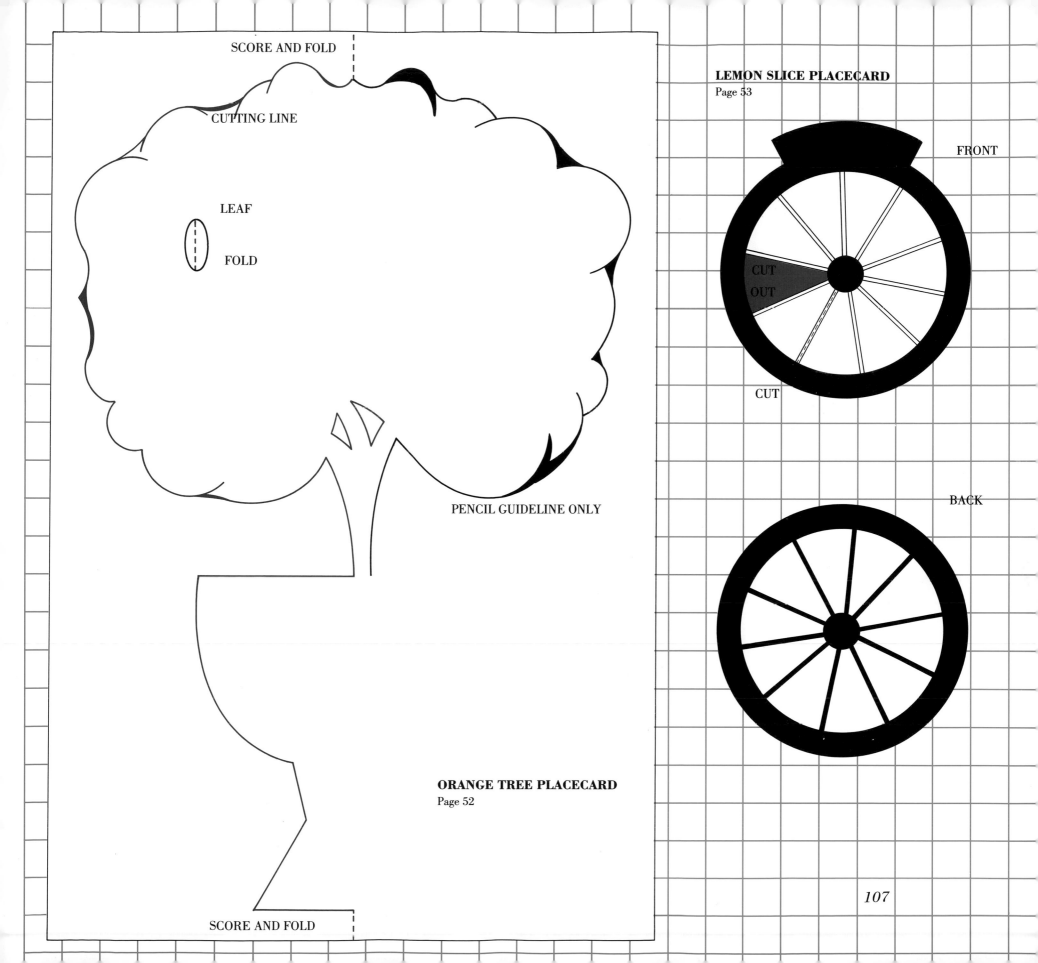

SCORE AND FOLD

CUTTING LINE

LEAF

FOLD

PENCIL GUIDELINE ONLY

ORANGE TREE PLACECARD
Page 52

SCORE AND FOLD

LEMON SLICE PLACECARD
Page 53

FRONT

CUT OUT

CUT

BACK

107

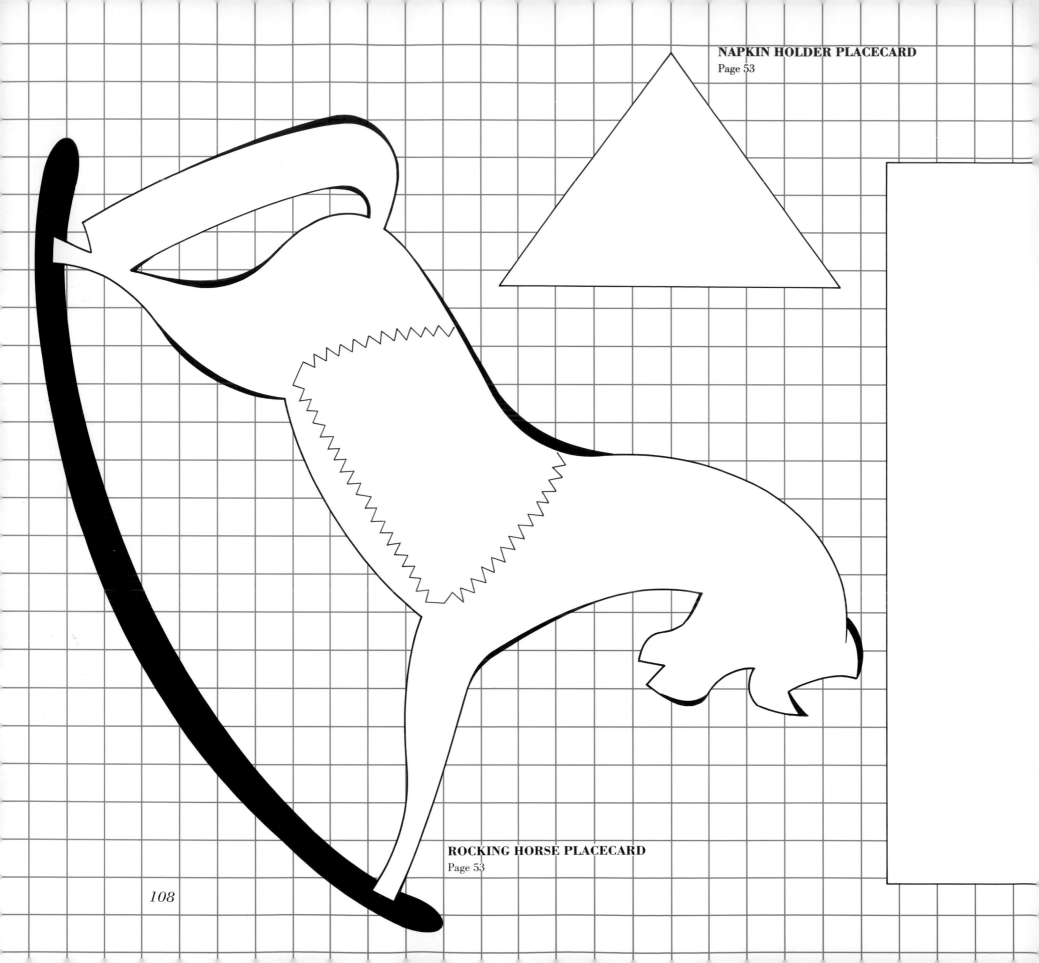

NAPKIN HOLDER PLACECARD
Page 53

ROCKING HORSE PLACECARD
Page 53

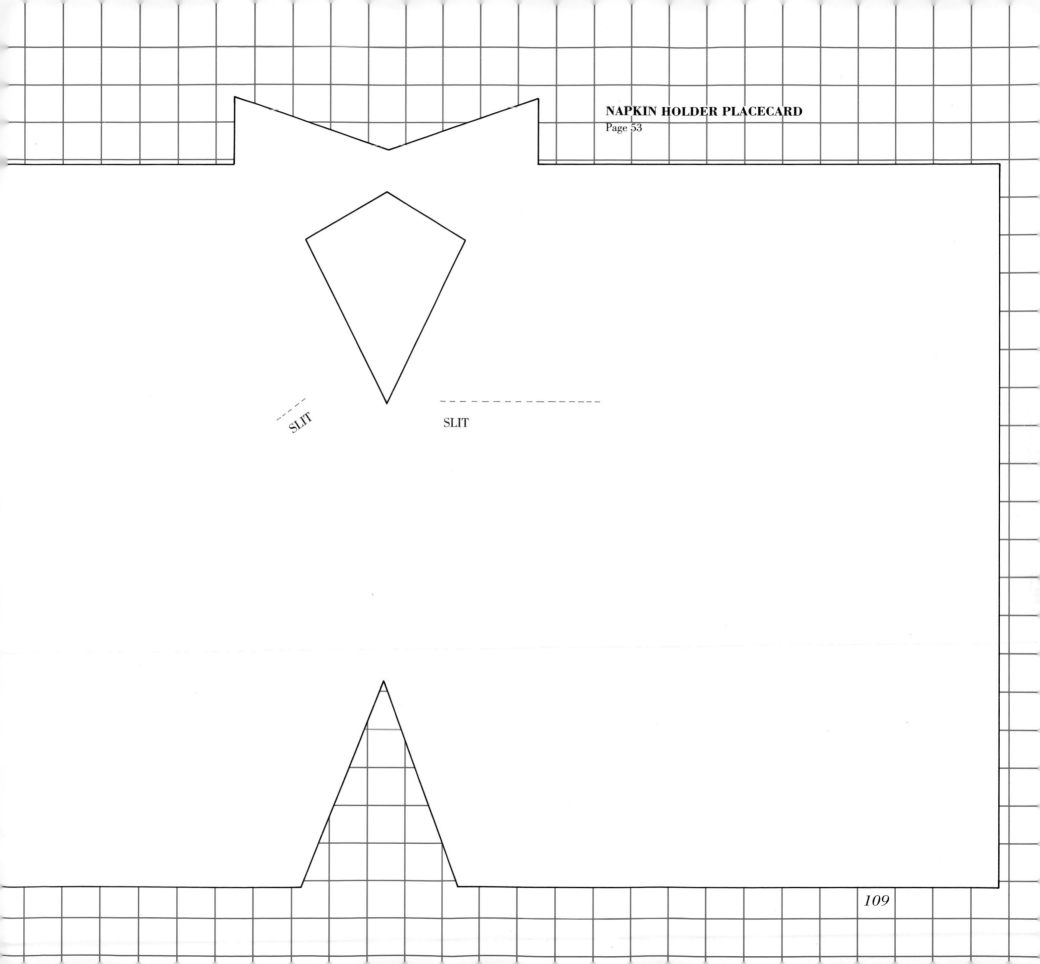

SLIT

SLIT

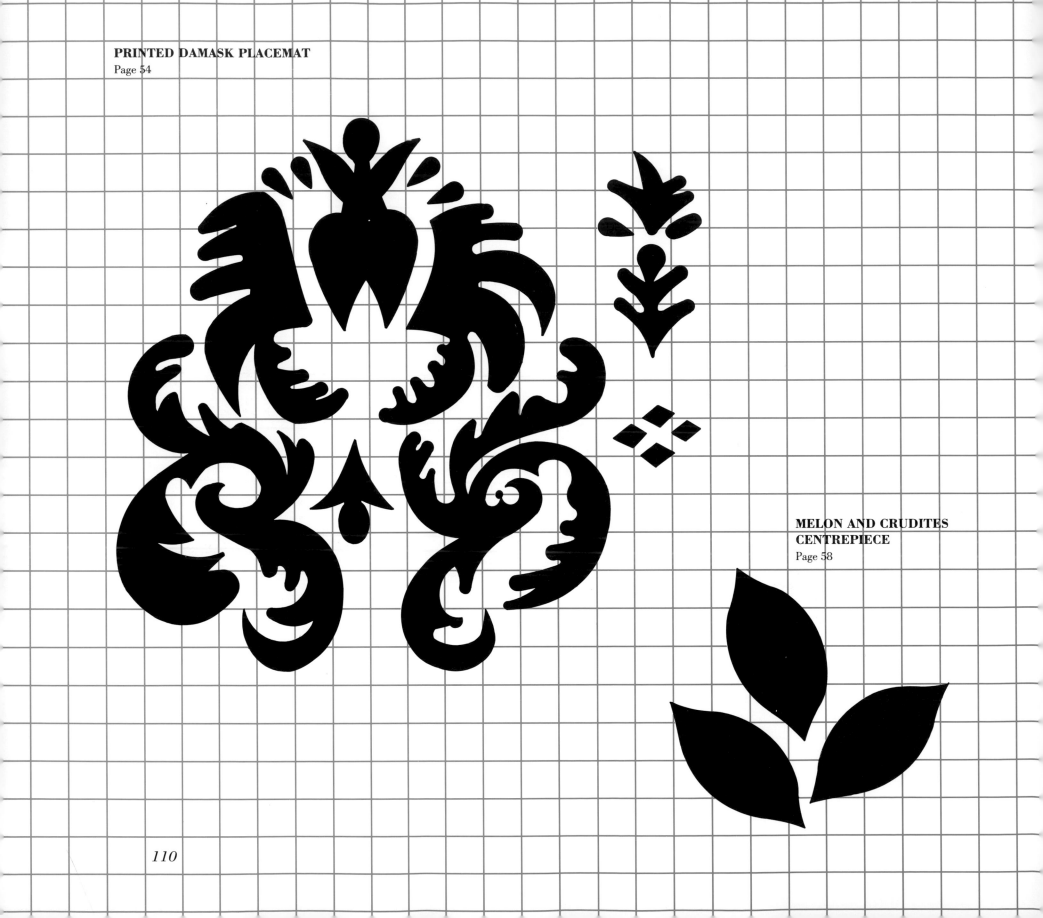

PRINTED DAMASK PLACEMAT
Page 54

**MELON AND CRUDITES
CENTREPIECE**
Page 58

110

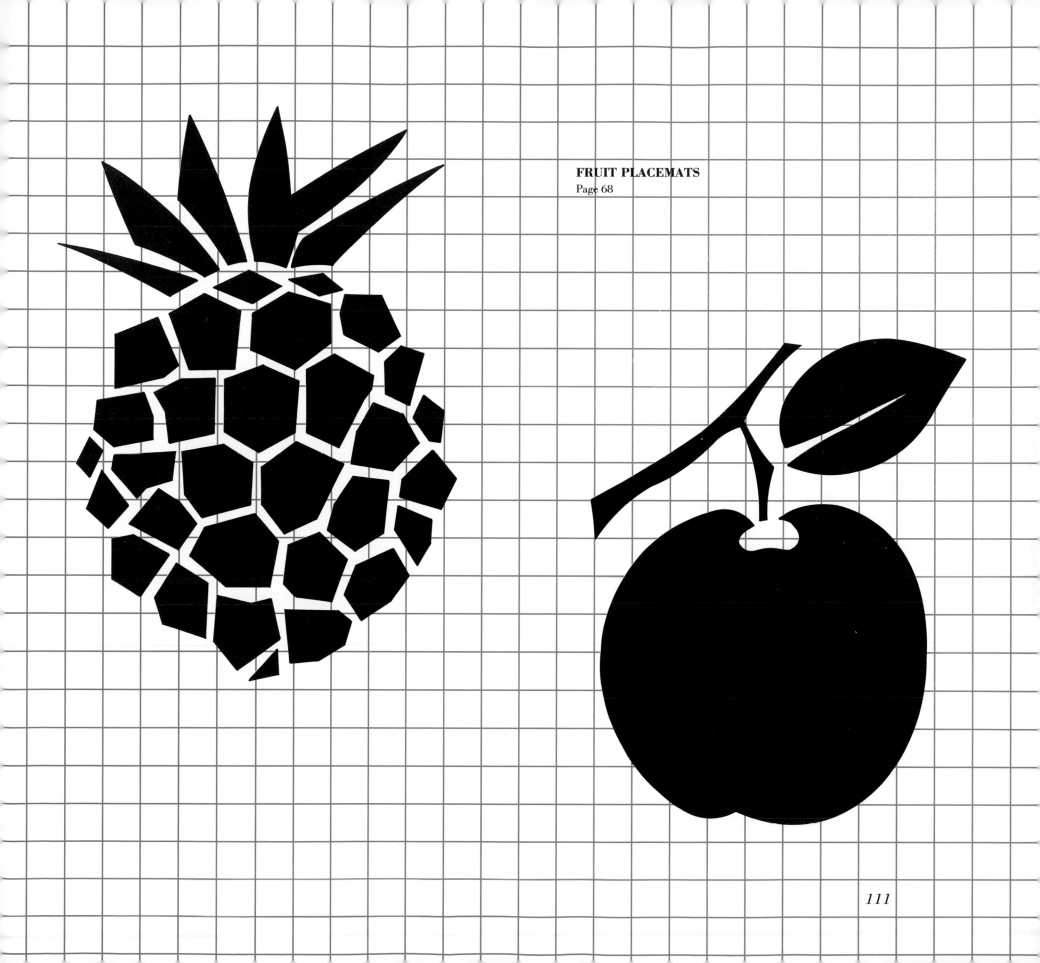

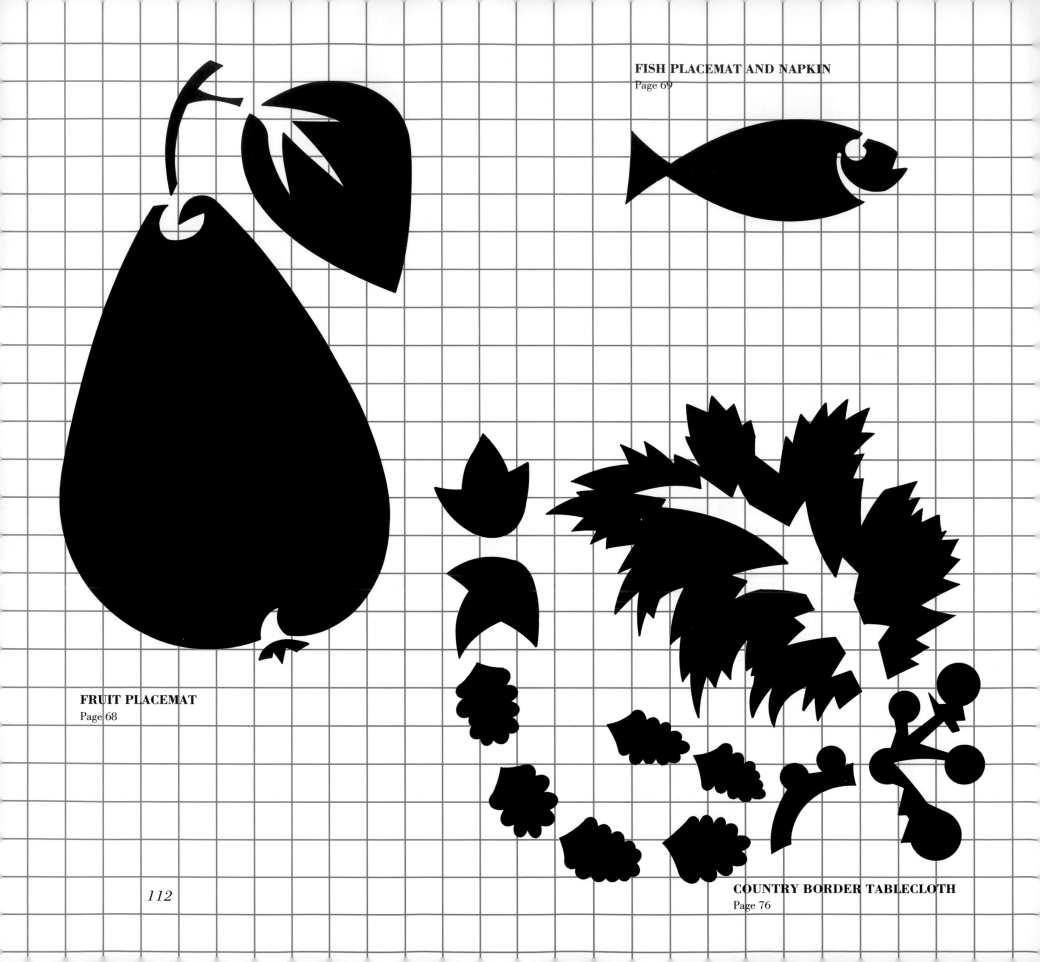

FISH PLACEMAT AND NAPKIN
Page 69

FRUIT PLACEMAT
Page 68

112

COUNTRY BORDER TABLECLOTH
Page 76

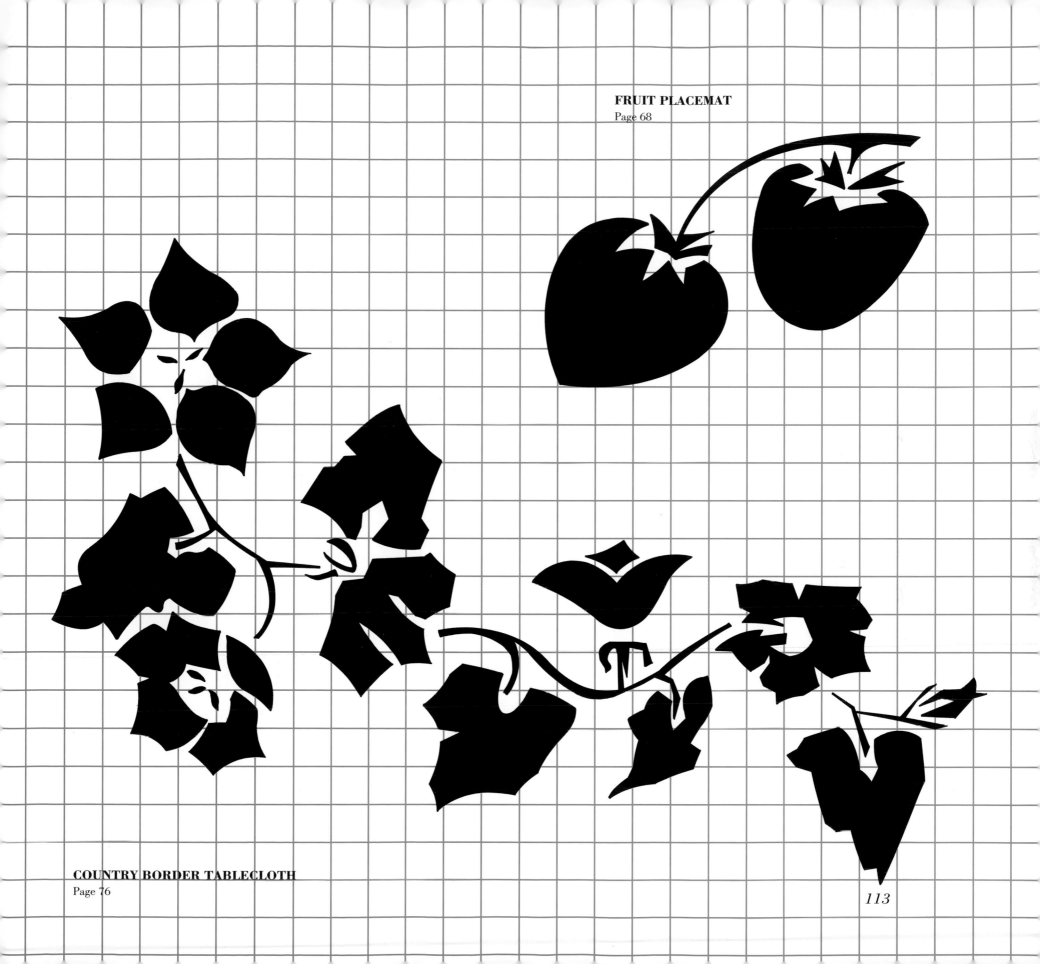

FRUIT PLACEMAT
Page 68

COUNTRY BORDER TABLECLOTH
Page 76

CUTTING LINE FOR WADDING AND LINING. ADD 2.5 CM (1 IN) SEAM ALLOWANCE FOR 'TOP' FABRIC.

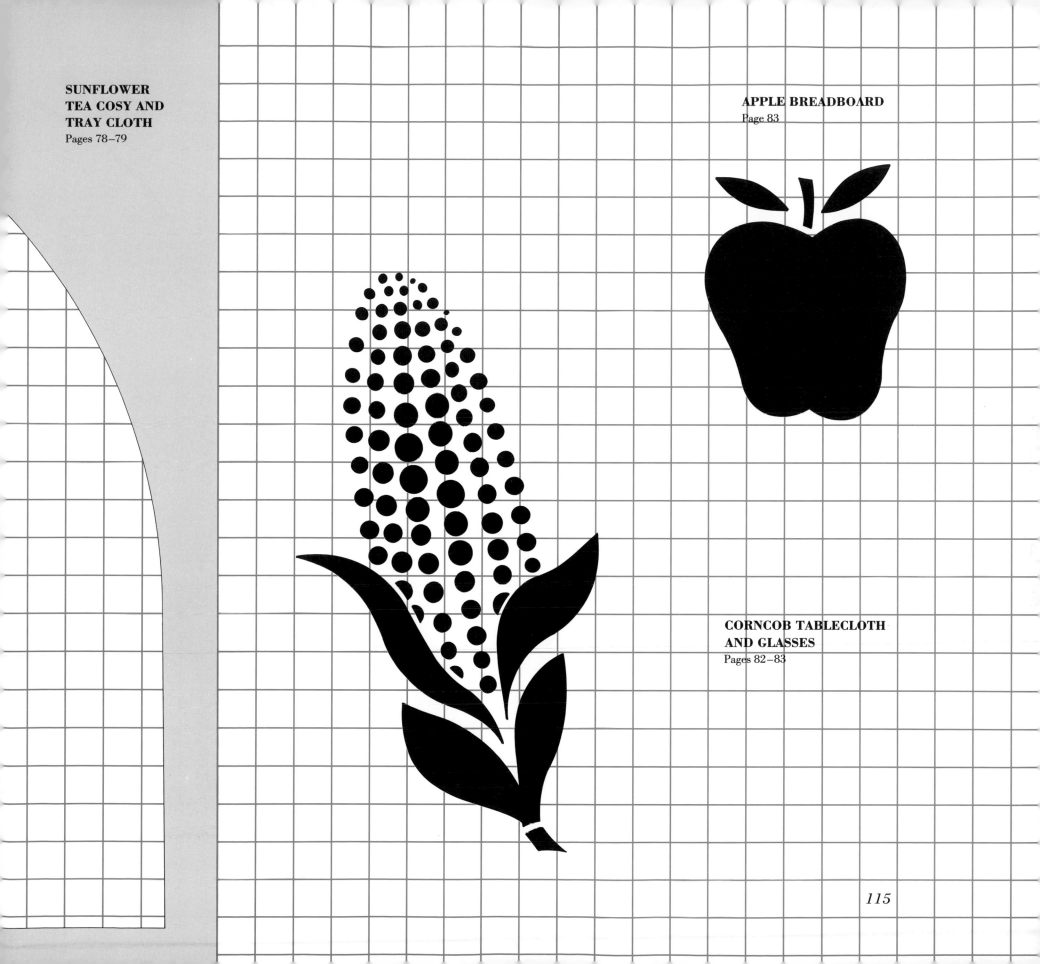

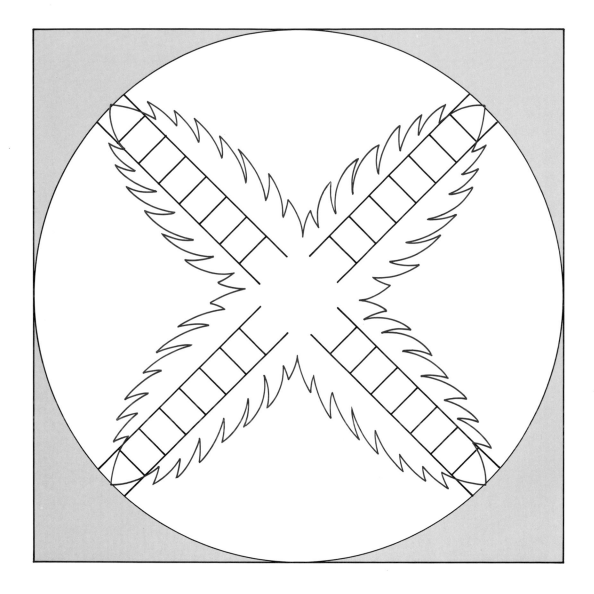

JUNGLE LEAVES AND SNAKES AND LADDERS TABLECLOTHS
Pages 98–99, 100–101

116

SLIT

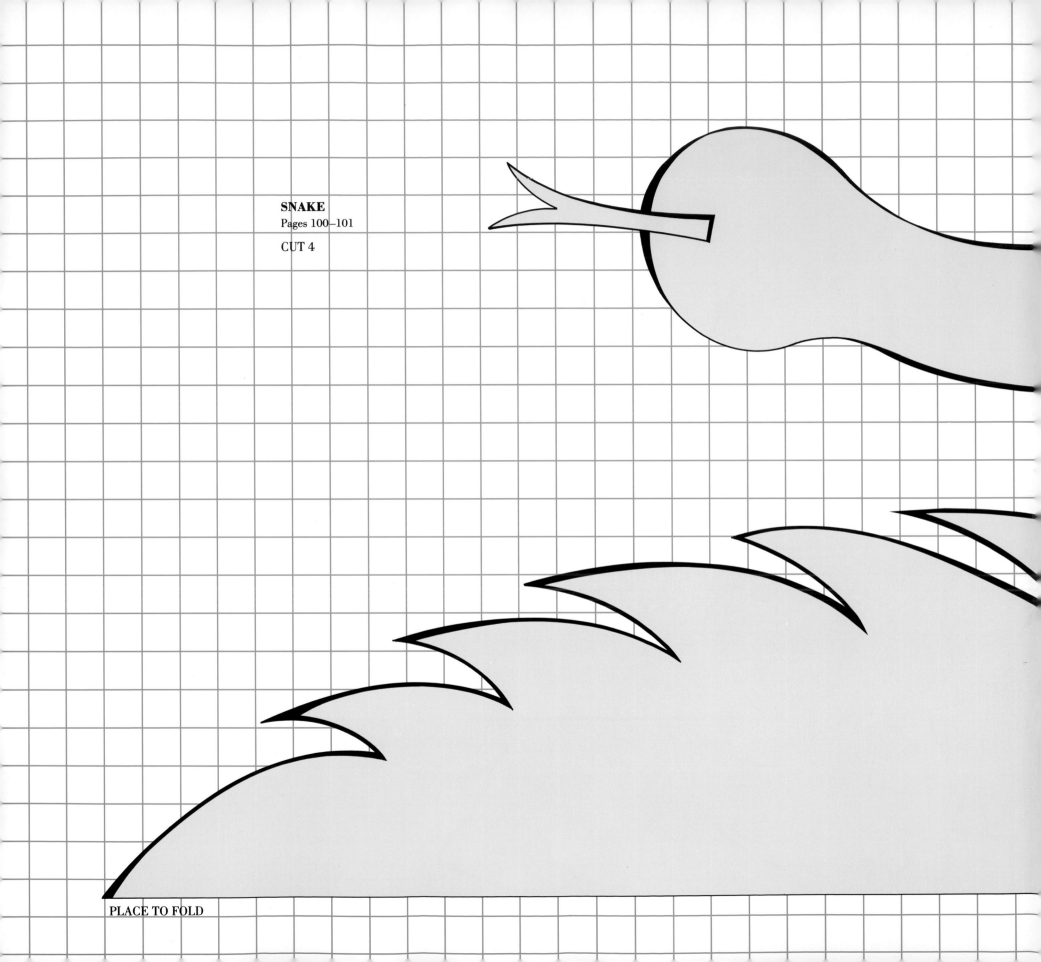

SNAKE
Pages 100–101

CUT 4

PLACE TO FOLD

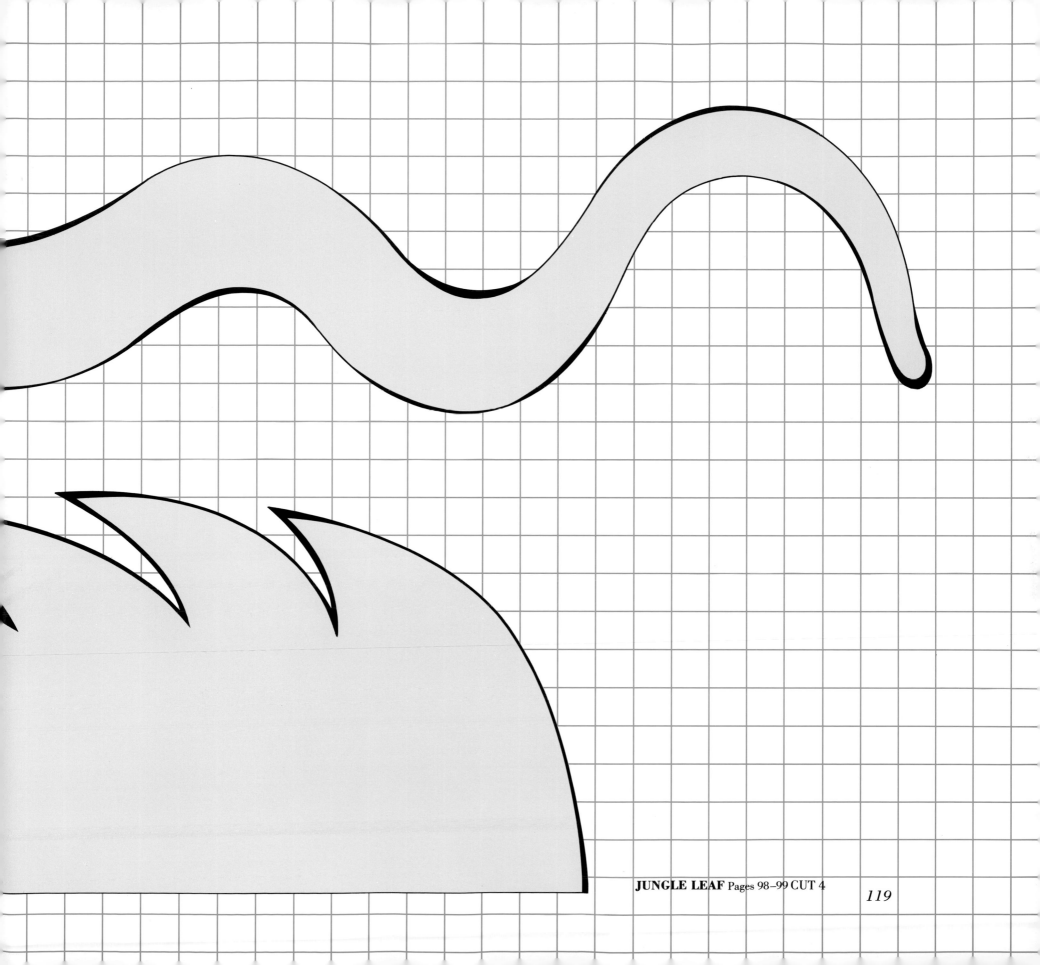

JUNGLE LEAF Pages 98–99 CUT 4

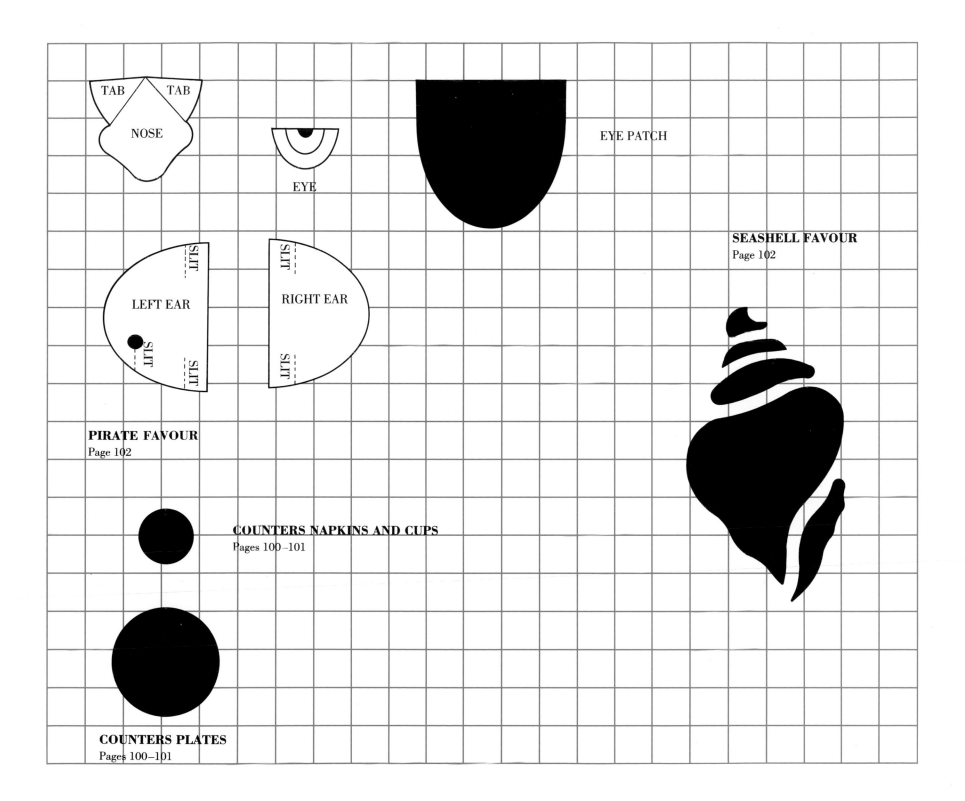

TAB TAB

NOSE

EYE

EYE PATCH

SEASHELL FAVOUR
Page 102

SLIT

LEFT EAR

RIGHT EAR

SLIT

SLIT

SLIT

PIRATE FAVOUR
Page 102

COUNTERS NAPKINS AND CUPS
Pages 100–101

COUNTERS PLATES
Pages 100–101

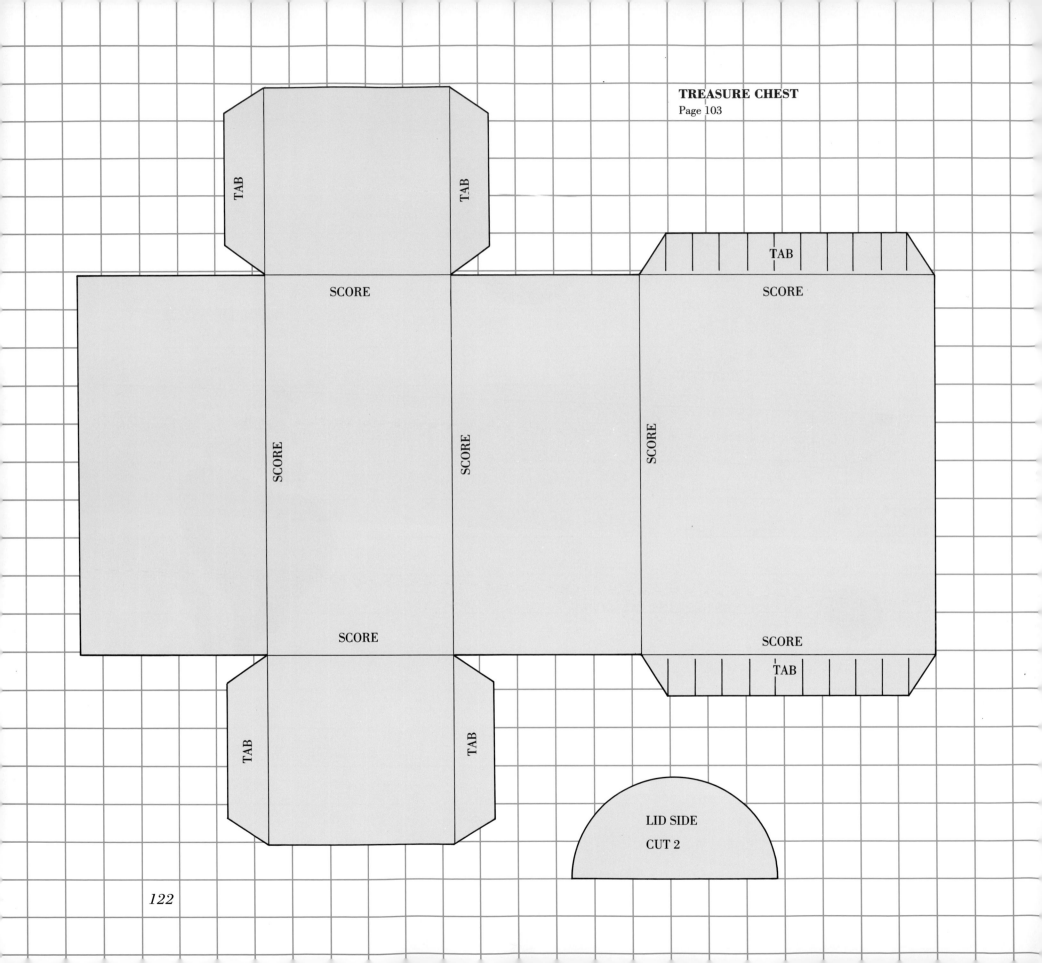

TREASURE CHEST
Page 103

TAB

TAB

SCORE

SCORE

SCORE

SCORE

TAB

TAB

SCORE

TAB

TAB

TAB

SCORE

SCORE

LID SIDE

CUT 2

122

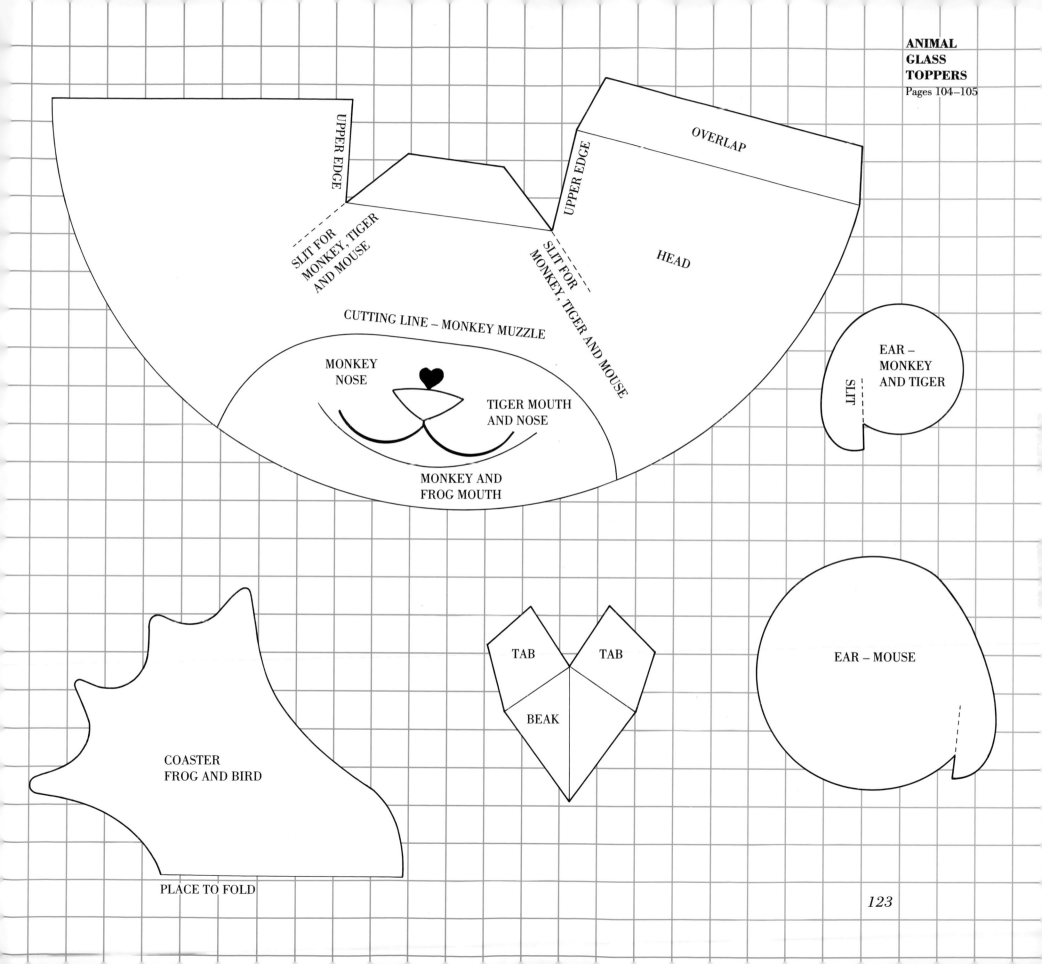

UPPER EDGE

OVERLAP

SLIT FOR
MONKEY, TIGER
AND MOUSE

UPPER EDGE

SLIT FOR
MONKEY, TIGER AND MOUSE

HEAD

CUTTING LINE – MONKEY MUZZLE

MONKEY
NOSE

TIGER MOUTH
AND NOSE

MONKEY AND
FROG MOUTH

EAR –
MONKEY
AND TIGER

SLIT

COASTER
FROG AND BIRD

TAB

TAB

BEAK

EAR – MOUSE

PLACE TO FOLD

123

AUTHOR'S ACKNOWLEDGEMENTS

Heartfelt thanks to the following who throughout the creative process provided information, materials, advice, and above all friendship: Tiina, Bertil, Bianca, Catja and Joni Barck; Mimosa Makela; Lillian Rothberg; Heli Sarka and Siv Linney; Mags, Dave, Anna and Alex Healey; Mary Fitzmaurice and Patricia Monahan; Keith, Andrew, Angus and Kate at T. Vintiners and Co.; and finally my mum.

PUBLISHER'S ACKNOWLEDGEMENTS

We are most grateful to Thomas Goode and Son (worldwide suppliers of tableware), 19 South Audley Street, London, and to Wedgwood, 158 Regent Street, London, for their generous help in supplying china and glass.
Thanks are also due to the following companies: ABC Linens, New York; Archetique Enterprises Inc., New York; Boots The Chemists; Borovick Fabrics Ltd; Calico Fabrics; China Regency, New York; Cowling and Wilcox Ltd; Cromartie Hobbycraft Ltd; Fortnum and Mason; Habitat; Halfords; Harrods; Lakeland Plastics Ltd; John Lewis plc; Liberty; Macys, New York; M. and J. Trimmings Co., New York; The Monogrammed Linen Co.; Paperchase; The Pier; Roundhouse Fruit (dried flowers); Safeway plc; J. Sainsbury plc; T. Vintiners and Co.; Warmerdam Nurseries, Enfield, (floristry supplies); Woolworths plc.
The following individuals have also kindly lent table items:
Nicola Dent, Ann Hamlyn, Matthew Hamlyn, Neil Sutherland.

Contributors: Mary Hamlyn, Cheryl Owen, Annette Claxton, Alison Jewell, Jo Finnis
Editor: Geraldine Christy
Design and styling: Mary Hamlyn
Photography: Steve Tanner, Neil Sutherland
Photographic direction: Mary Hamlyn, Jo Finnis, Geraldine Christy
Illustration: Geoff Denney Associates, Phil Gorton
Production: Ruth Arthur, Sally Connolly, Neil Randles, Jonathan Tickner
Director of production: Gerald Hughes